DDC

Computer
Troubleshooting

© Haynes Publishing 2004
Reprinted 2004 and 2006
Second edition published 2008

Published by: Haynes Publishing
Sparkford, Yeovil, Somerset BA22 7JJ
Tel: 01963 442030 Fax: 01963 440001
Int. tel: +44 1963 442030 Fax: +44 1963 440001
E-mail: sales@haynes.co.uk
Website: www.haynes.co.uk

British Library Cataloguing in Publication Data:
A catalogue record for this book is available from the British Library

ISBN 978 1 84425 517 7

Printed in Britain by J. H. Haynes & Co. Ltd, Sparkford

Throughout this book, trademarked names are used. Rather than put a
trademark symbol after every occurrence of a trademarked name, we use
the names in an editorial fashion only, and to the benefit of the trademark
owner, with no intention of infringement of the trademark. Where such
designations appear in this book, they have been printed with initial caps.

Whilst we at J. H. Haynes & Co. Ltd. strive to ensure the accuracy and
completeness of the information in this book, it is provided entirely at the
risk of the user. Neither the company nor the author can accept liability
for any errors, omissions or damage resulting therefrom. In particular,
users should be aware that component and accessory manufacturers, and
software providers, can change specifications without notice, thus
appropriate professional advice should always be sought.

Haynes

Computer Troubleshooting

The complete step-by-step guide to
diagnosing and fixing common PC problems

Haynes ®

Kyle MacRae &
Gary Marshall

Second Edition

Contents

Introduction

The best thing about PCs is their versatility, which makes them as happy editing your home video or playing games as they are doing dull office work. However, that very versatility is also a problem. When you consider the huge range of hardware and software components that PCs need to support, it's not a surprise that they pack up from time to time. In fact, it's amazing that they ever work at all.

The golden rule of computing is that sooner or later, something will go wrong. It might be a massive system crash that wipes out Windows or, more likely, a small but extremely annoying and frustrating bug. Bits of kit that worked perfectly well yesterday may pack up or play dead today, mysterious error messages may scare you silly, or Windows may seem to forget your settings and revert to the factory defaults.

The good news is that fixing computer problems is easy. The trick is to know what to look for, by checking possible causes and eliminating them until you find – and fix – the problem. When you know what's playing up, whether it's a bit of hardware, an unruly program or a good-old-fashioned bug, fixing it is usually simple. So that's the approach we'll take here.

This is a manual for anyone who wants to recover gracefully from a computer problem without spending stacks of time or, worse, money. Even the biggest problems can usually be fixed with the minimum of fuss so, for example, if part of your PC packs up, it's easy to replace it. Notice we say replace and not repair: in the majority of cases it's easier and cheaper to simply swap out a duff component or hardware driver than try to fix it.

Hardware repair is seldom an option; replacement is the answer.

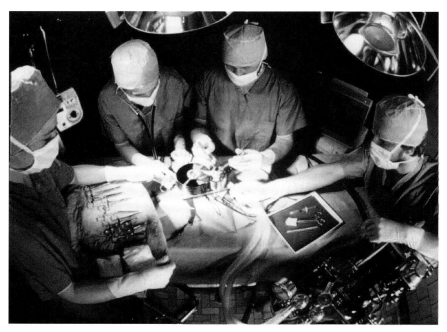

Is there an alternative to DIY troubleshooting? There is. In fact, there are several alternatives. You could simply grin and bear it, letting the problem recur until it drives you daft; you could take it to a shop and pay expensive hourly rates for a technician to fix it; you could spend all day on a premium-rate helpline listening to someone reading from a script and asking 'have you turned it off and switched it back on again?' or you could send your entire system back to the manufacturer and pray you'll get it back before it's obsolete. We think it's better to go the DIY route, not just because it'll save you money but because it's usually the quickest, easiest and most effective way to solve computer problems – and to save your sanity.

KenPyne

Frustration is natural but a cool head, patience and logic usually get you further.

How to use this book

 Single click on the left mouse button

 Double click on the left mouse button

 Single click on the right mouse button

 Check or uncheck this option by clicking the left mouse button

 Type the following text on your keyboard

Wherever possible, we'll show you exactly what to do with screenshots and plain English descriptions.

We'll occasionally use the term 'Windows 9x' in this book as a handy shorthand for 'Windows 95, Windows 98 and Windows Millennium Edition', as these versions of Windows all work in the same way. With Windows 2000, Windows XP and Windows Vista things are rather different, so we'll look at them separately from Windows 9x.

Screen examples

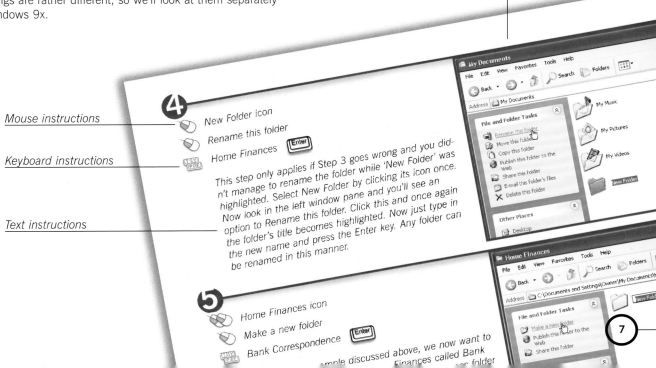

Mouse instructions

Keyboard instructions

Text instructions

④ New Folder icon

Rename this folder

Home Finances [Enter]

This step only applies if Step 3 goes wrong and you did-n't manage to rename the folder while 'New Folder' was highlighted. Select New Folder by clicking its icon once. Now look in the left window pane and you'll see an option to Rename this folder. Click this and once again the folder's title becomes highlighted. Now just type in the new name and press the Enter key. Any folder can be renamed in this manner.

⑤ Home Finances icon

Make a new folder

Bank Correspondence [Enter]

...mple discussed above, we now want to ...Finances called Bank ...folder

start

TROUBLESHOOTING

Windows woes

Windows acts as a middleman between you and your computer, so it makes sure all the hardware works happily and that your programs do what they're supposed to do. As long as hardware and software firms make sure their products are 100% compatible with Windows, everything should work perfectly well. And most of the time, that's exactly what happens. Sometimes, though, it all goes to pot – and this chapter shows you how to fix it when it does.

PART 1

Overview

There are two kinds of computer problems: hardware ones and software ones. Hardware problems are usually very simple (as we'll see later in this manual) but tracking down software glitches can be a head-banging, expletive-deleted pain in the neck. Why can't our computers just work?

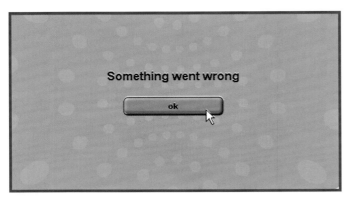

This is way too colourful to be a Windows error message, but singing about bad news doesn't turn it into good news.

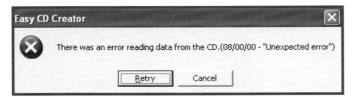

If a CD cannot be read it is probably dirty or damaged, so why not say so? And are not all errors unexpected?

In this message, Windows admits to failing to handle an exception (an error by any other name), but we are not told what it was or how to prevent it happening again. A 'Sorry' button would seem more appropriate than 'OK'.

Imagine if you bought a pair of trousers and one leg fell off or if you discovered that the blockbuster book you've just picked up doesn't have all the pages. You'd be furious and demand a refund. And yet when our computers do something annoying or refuse to do anything at all, we're expected to fix them ourselves. In any other industry we'd be heading for the factory with flaming torches, but with computers we're expected to tolerate programs that act unpredictably, run on some computers but not others, and which occasionally go into a huge huff if you ask them to work with another company's products.

Why don't things work properly?

To be fair, few – if any – companies sell hardware or software that doesn't work properly. The problem is the mind-boggling range of computers, programs and add-ons that we use. Firms' products need to work on computers from Dell, Toshiba, Fujitsu and Sony; they need to work with chips from Intel and from AMD; they need to play happily on desktops, laptops, tablet computers and mini-PCs; and they need to cope with a dizzying range of add-ons: hundreds of hard disks, hundreds of mice, hundreds of keyboards – you get the idea. And if that wasn't enough, software that was written two years ago needs to work with software that was only released last week.

Of course, we can't expect computer companies to see into the future but we can expect them to make sure their products work with Windows. That way, if we keep Windows up to date and install any software updates from the people who make our hardware and our programs, our PCs should be happy PCs. Most of the time, that's exactly what happens.

Unfortunately, from time to time problems do occur. An unforeseeable conflict between your graphics card and a Windows update could make your PC throw a fit, or the combination of three perfectly reliable programs running at the same time could cause a 'perfect storm' that brings your system to its knees. And what does your PC do then? Usually, it gives you an error message so obscure that even the people who made the program aren't entirely sure what the problem is. We've scattered some examples across this introduction to show you the sort of messages we all have to deal with.

It's not all bad, though. Even the most opaque error message can give you valuable information, especially if you can get online to see how other users have solved the same problem.

Walloping Windows problems

Whenever you do anything on your PC, Windows handles it. Want to view a digital photo? Windows talks to the hard disk, locates the file, copies it into memory and then sends it through your PC's video hardware so you can see it on screen. When you click on the Print button, Windows spots the mouse click, translates the picture into something your printer can understand and asks for a printout. And when you email the photo to a friend, Windows takes care of the digital postage and packing to ensure that your picture travels over the internet to reach the right person.

Unfortunately, Windows can be damaged. Crucial files can be deleted by accident, viruses can make it do strange things and, because it's so complicated, the odd bug can be found lurking in an obscure corner. If any of those things makes Windows go wrong, the effects can be dramatic. If something happens to Windows' printing engine, no programs will be able to print. If its internet settings get mucked up then no programs can access the internet. If something happens to its multimedia features, your CDs, movies or MP3s could be silent, and so on. Worst of all, if something really bad happens and Windows' essential system files get damaged, your PC might not even start.

That's why we'll look at Windows woes first. Over the following pages, we'll discover the most common kinds of Windows problems, how to fix them and how to make sure they don't rear their ugly heads again. And if all else fails, we'll show you how you can fix even the most badly damaged copy of Windows by reinstalling it.

Other than this book, the single most useful troubleshooting tool you can have is access to the internet. Online – provided you know where to look – you'll find the answers to almost everything, along with downloadable tools that can sort out problems or fix broken bits of software. If your own PC won't start or connect to the internet, it's a very good idea to borrow a friend's PC, use the office PC during your lunch break or wander down to the library or an internet café. It's even better if the PC you borrow has a CD burner or a USB port into which you can stick a USB pen drive, as some files can be rather big.

The second most useful Windows troubleshooting tool is the Windows installation CD or DVD itself and any installation CDs or DVDs that came along with your system. If you have a laptop, you might find that you didn't get any discs at all, in which case you'll find a utility on your computer that will make backup, installation or restore discs for you. The time to use this utility is when your laptop is being lovely, ideally when it's just been delivered. You never know when you might need those discs.

A puzzling one, this. Are we to assume that Windows has successfully created a problem but failed to create an object?

A peerless error message that tells you precisely nothing, not even the name of the program with apparently AWOL code.

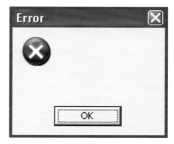

Windows XP is the most helpful version of Windows so far but, as this message shows, it too has its off days.

How serious could this mysterious error have been if Windows fixed it unaided and why tell us? Does Microsoft expect a pat on the back?

If your software carries this or a similar logo, you know that it should work flawlessly with Windows. However, that doesn't entirely rule out conflicts with other programs, particularly if they haven't been developed in similarly strict accordance with Microsoft guidelines.

An honest error message at last. Shame we had to make it up.

Identifying the problem

This section is devoted to identifying what, if anything, is wrong with the current state of Windows on your computer. It describes symptoms and causes, and offers some tips that might point you towards a solution. You will find step-by-step help for the most common problems starting in the next section (see p17).

Human error

Most problems with Windows generate some sort of error message. If you know how to interpret these messages, they can be directly or indirectly helpful in isolating problems, but when you see an error message you shouldn't immediately assume the worst. It could be that the message results from human error – yours!

You can't delete a file if it is currently open in a program or in use by Windows Explorer.

Trying to save a file onto a floppy disk when there is no disk in the drive is a common mistake. Another is trying to delete a file using Windows Explorer while a program is using it. It is impossible to say for certain which is the most common mistake, but one that we have all made is typing illegal symbols when trying to save a file. Windows reserves nine symbols (* ? / \ < | > : ") for its own use and won't tolerate any of them in a filename. In most versions of Windows the error message relating to filenames is one of the more helpful ones because it lists the nine unacceptable symbols, but Windows XP goes one step further and actually refuses to let you type any of the symbols while renaming a file in Windows Explorer.

Typically, warnings relating to human errors are displayed in standard Windows message boxes containing a cross in a red circle or an exclamation point in a yellow triangle. These have no particular meaning other than to catch your attention. Whatever sort of human error you make, once you have clicked the OK button to continue you can correct your mistake and carry on as if nothing had happened.

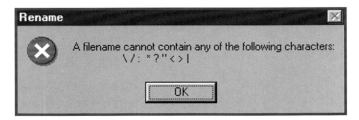

The Rename error message from Windows 9x helpfully tells you what you have done wrong while this Save As message thrown up by Windows XP merely condemns your mistake.

Damaged programs

One way programs become damaged is when computers are turned off without closing down properly. Sometimes this is unavoidable, as in the case of hardware failure or an unexpected power cut, and sometimes you have no alternative but to hit the power or reset switch yourself when Windows refuses to respond to the mouse or keyboard. Programs are also made unusable by loading them into a word processor or a spreadsheet and re-saving them. While you are unlikely to do this yourself, others who use your computer might do so inadvertently.

We have never seen a damaged program produce a clear error message saying *This program is fatally damaged – please reinstall it*. Instead, Windows will try to run the program and then deliver an error message telling you the program is not a valid Win32 application. In effect, this tells you the program is thoroughly broken.

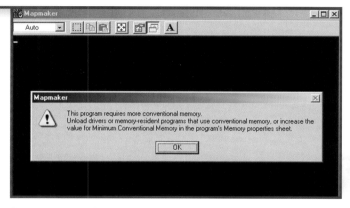

The appearance of this message over an MS-DOS box is a sure sign that the program – in this case, Mapmaker – is damaged beyond repair. Windows is merely confused.

Unfortunately, damaged programs sometimes generate spurious error messages that lead you astray. For example, Windows sometimes thinks that a damaged program is a DOS program and tries to run it in an MS-DOS window. When it cannot, it displays a message telling you to make more conventional memory available or tinker with the program's properties sheet. This will waste a great deal of your time but it won't get you anywhere; a Windows program will never run under DOS, however often you try. Simply reinstall it.

If you frequently suffer from corrupted programs and you are scrupulous about switching off properly, it is worth checking your hard disk for physical damage or a mangled filing system.

Before checking for disk errors in Windows XP, close all other programs.

In Windows 98 and Windows Me,

- Start
- Programs
- Accessories
- System Tools
- ScanDisk

and run the utility in 'thorough' mode.

In Windows XP, right-click drive *C:* to examine its properties, look in the Tools tab and click the Check Now button within the Error-checking section.

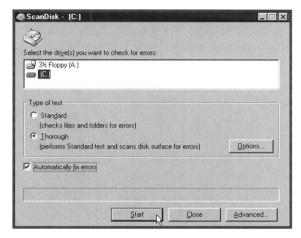

ScanDisk can identify and, in future, avoid 'bad' areas on a hard disk.

Fatal exceptions

A 'fatal exception' is not the title of a steamy Hollywood movie, but rather a type of Windows error from which there is no recovery. It is mightily inconvenient because it forces you to reboot Windows and lose anything you were working on.

The typical manifestation of a fatal exception in Windows 98/Me is a text message on a blue background. This is the so-called Blue Screen of Death (presumably named because there is no escape from it). There is a *Press any key to continue* option at the bottom of the blue screen but this is either an impenetrable Microsoft joke or wishful thinking. A reboot is inevitable so reach for the reset button – and hope that you saved any open documents recently.

A fatal exception is a special type of memory error. They can be caused by defective or loose memory chips, or by badly written programs that try to use memory reserved for other programs.

If the cause is bad memory chips, the errors will occur randomly regardless of what you are doing in Windows and you will need to identify and replace the faulty memory module (see p153); but if the cause is a badly written program, you should be able to make the fatal exception recur by repeating the same set of actions. Once you know which program is causing the problem, you can look for a patch or update on the company's website. Or, of course, uninstall it.

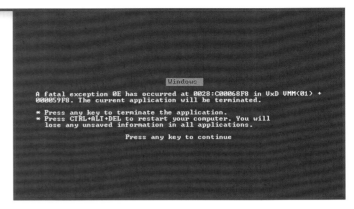

Fatal exceptions are only fatal to the current session. They can be fixed once you know which program is causing them.

Stop errors

The Windows 2000 and Windows XP version of the blue screen of death is the 'stop error'. It has a wider range of causes, including conflicts between drivers and poor interaction between Windows and third-party anti-virus software.

Unlike a blue screen in Windows 98 and Windows Me, a stop error screen contains coded information about the cause of the error in the top two lines. This makes it markedly easier to find help in the Microsoft Knowledge Base or on independent websites. Usually a web search for the first stop number from the top line (ignore the four numbers in brackets) together with the description of the error given at the start of the second line will tell you all you need to know (see also p54).

The Recovery Console in Windows 2000 and Windows XP is another way of identifying and fixing stop errors (see p28).

This is the sort of stop error (basically, a friendlier 'blue screen of death') produced by Windows 2000 and Windows XP.

Illegal operations

These are not violations of medical ethics or clandestine sorties into foreign lands; an illegal operation in Windows 9x is when a program tries to do something that doesn't make sense to Windows. Rather than risk the stability of the entire system, Windows terminates the program.

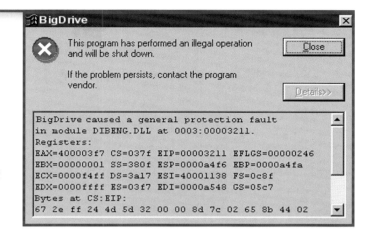

Illegal operations don't force you to close down your computer but it makes sense to save any work in progress and reboot, just in case.

The cause could be a poorly written program that trips over its own feet but it is just as likely to be a conflict with another program or damage to a Windows system file.

For clues, click the Details button in the Illegal Operation error message box. You will see a message that says something along the lines of *Starview executed an invalid instruction in module starview.exe at 0000:0063fa88.*

The raw numbers are completely unhelpful but the program name is a clue. Possible solutions include updating, reinstalling or patching the program – in this case, Starview – which necessitates a trip to the software developer's website.

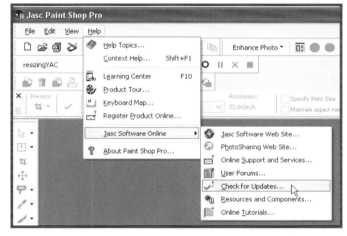

Check for program updates regularly to keep software running sweetly.

The easiest route there, incidentally, is often through a shortcut on a program's Help menu. But if the fault lies with Windows, you may need to restore a Windows file from the installation CD (see p36). Fortunately, if the problem is a common one related to a mainstream product, you will almost certainly find a solution on the web (see p52).

Missing DLLs

Very few programs come as a single executable file these days. To make them easier to manage and faster to load, they are chopped up into smaller modules. When you install a program called, say, Superwrite, you get not only Superwrite.exe but also lots of support files, many of which will be dynamic linked libraries.

Dynamic linked libraries are supplied as files with the extension DLL, and they are treated exactly like real-world libraries by the programs that use them. They contain programming code that can be borrowed and used on demand. If the DLL is not there when it is needed, or if it has been damaged, a program will stop dead in its tracks. Because Windows itself relies on a number of DLLs, the impact of DLL-related problems can be far-reaching.

DLL errors affect all versions of Windows. This message occurred in Windows Me.

Even more errors...

This quick rundown of common errors has been far from exhaustive. You may also expect to suffer invalid page faults, which are memory allocation errors caused by faulty RAM chips or by one program claiming the memory reserved for another program (Windows is supposed to prevent this happening but doesn't always succeed). If you get a page fault you cannot trace, check that your hard disk is not full. Even 100MB of free space might not be enough.

General Protection Faults are the most common type of fatal exception. When they are not caused by third-party software, they are usually the result of using out-of-date or inappropriate drivers. Use selective start-up techniques in Safe Mode (see p22) to identify the problem driver so you can replace it.

Being able to categorise errors is an interesting party trick but it is less useful than being able to pick out the important clue from an error situation and track down the solution. Above all, when faced with an error message, don't panic. This means you should avoid taking drastic steps like formatting a hard disk until other solutions have been tried.

Unfortunately, Windows will lead you astray with messages like the one in Windows 9x that says *Error loading Kernel. You must reinstall Windows*. As described on p38, the problem can usually be fixed by copying the single *kernel32.dll* file from the installation CD, which is much faster than reinstalling Windows and doesn't mess up your Windows settings.

To turn any of the thousands of numerically-coded Windows error codes into plain English, try the helpful, free program called 'Error messages for Windows' available from www.gregorybraun.com.

How do I know when my computer has a problem?

● Your computer will not even start.

● Your computer will start but it will not load Windows.

● You receive an error message when you load Windows.

● Windows starts only in Safe Mode.

● Windows stops working after a period of time, with or without a blue screen or other message being displayed.

● Your computer refuses to perform certain tasks, such as printing or communicating with USB accessories.

● Your computer is underperforming. Perhaps it runs slowly all the time or maybe it slows down when performing a particular task.

● The screen picture is unacceptable (flickering, distorted or the wrong size).

● Sound output is distorted or missing altogether.

● Windows will not close down.

Crashes and freezes

A crash is when Windows literally falls apart. Some or all of the programs stop running and often the screen becomes corrupted with graphical fragments that can look like TV interference. You are unable to close down normally even though you might still have limited use of the mouse and keyboard. A freeze is less dramatic but just as debilitating: Windows simply stops responding to anything you do with the mouse or keyboard, even though everything looks OK on the screen.

In either event, your only recourse is to do what you are not supposed to: turn off the power without first closing down Windows. You will lose any unsaved work but you won't permanently damage your computer. When Windows restarts, you will have to wait while your hard disk is checked for errors. Usually such errors are repairable but if essential files have been damaged you will have to replace them or reinstall Windows.

This type of screen corruption is typical of a Windows crash. It doesn't necessarily indicate a video or graphics problem.

PART **1**

Windows will not start

The first thing many people think of when Windows won't even start is a virus, but in fact this is a remote possibility unless you have been running your computer without a virus scanner installed or if you have been foolishly ignoring its warnings to bring its virus signatures up to date.

The cause is far more likely to be a damaged or deleted Windows file, or it may be that a program you have installed has overwritten a Windows file with one of its own. However, it is best not to jump to conclusions when troubleshooting a computer that won't start. Instead, follow the procedures outlined below.

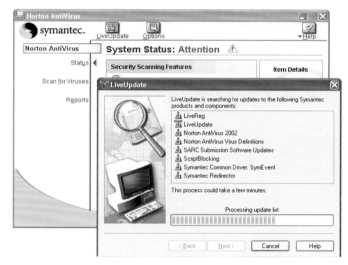

Any anti-virus program worth its salt will let you update its virus database online.

Rule out hardware problems

For help with hardware-related problems turn to Parts 3, 4 and 5. You will know if the problem is with Windows rather than the computer itself because your computer will make an effort to start: its lights will glow, its disks and fans will spin and something will be displayed on the monitor, even if it is only an Energy Star logo and a few lines of start-up messages.

If your computer remains more or less inert but beeps at you strangely (one long beep is normal but any combination of short beeps means hardware problems), the pattern of beeps can be interpreted by reference to your computer manual or to the website of its BIOS manufacturer.

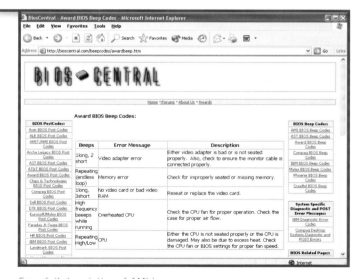

For a full description of AMI beep codes (and the beep codes for every other BIOS supplier) visit http://bioscentral.com.

Rule out the obvious

A computer can be configured to start directly from its hard disk or to first examine its floppy drive to see if it contains a disk and, if so, boot from that. If your computer is set up like this (which is perfectly normal), then make sure there is no floppy disk in the drive when you switch on. If there is you will get a message telling you to *Remove disks or other media*, or possibly the more cryptic *Non system disk or disk error*, or even the gloomy *Boot disk failure*. When you remove the floppy and press a key, your computer should boot from its hard disk in the usual way. If there is no offending disk in the floppy drive, it indicates that the system files on the hard disk are damaged or unreadable, at least temporarily. In these situations, always try switching off, waiting, and then rebooting before doing anything drastic. Sometimes it helps to let your computer cool down.

```
Boot disk failure
```

Not a sight to gladden the soul but it may be less serious than it sounds. Check your floppy drive for an errant disk.

Boot failure

The messages *Boot failure*, *Missing Operating System* and *General failure reading drive C* all indicate that your computer cannot start Windows from the hard disk because it cannot find certain system files. A disk with physical defects might generate identical error messages but the cause is more likely to be missing or damaged files.

If your computer uses Windows 98 or Windows Me, your first line of attack is to use a start-up floppy disk made within Windows (see p21) to attempt a repair. Restart your computer with the start-up floppy disk in the drive. When it has finished loading, type:

Sys C:

When you press the Enter key, this will reinstate the missing system files onto the hard disk and should result in a *System Transferred* message. Remove the floppy disk and try restarting your computer.

This trick doesn't work with the NT-based XP and 2000 versions of Windows because they are not reliant on MS-DOS. Instead, use the Windows Recovery Console (see p28).

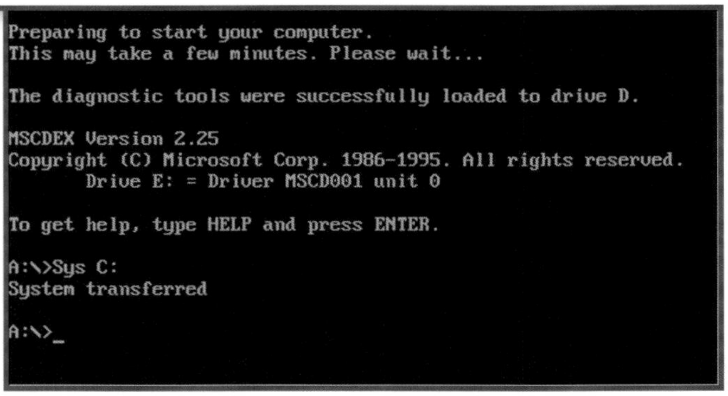

```
Preparing to start your computer.
This may take a few minutes. Please wait...

The diagnostic tools were successfully loaded to drive D.

MSCDEX Version 2.25
Copyright (C) Microsoft Corp. 1986-1995. All rights reserved.
     Drive E: = Driver MSCD001 unit 0

To get help, type HELP and press ENTER.

A:\>Sys C:
System transferred

A:\>_
```

It is important to use a start-up disk made with the same version of Windows as the one you are repairing.

Replacing missing or damaged files

When a computer boots successfully, it can still fail to load Windows if any of the Windows system files have been affected by a device or program that has been recently installed or uninstalled. Files can also be damaged or deleted by human hands, virus attack or as a result of switching off your computer without first closing down Windows.

Knowing which file is damaged or missing isn't usually a problem because when Windows fails to load it displays an error message indicating the source of the problem. This might be a text message on a black screen or one of the blue screens of death, from which there is no escape no matter what keys you press.

The files that are most prone to damage are 'virtual device drivers'. These have the extension VXD after their names. Using a program called *Extract.exe*, found on the Windows 98 and Windows Me start-up disks, you can extract the missing or damaged files from a Windows installation CD and place them in the correct location on your hard disk. In Windows XP, file extraction is performed from the Recovery Console as described on p29.

To replace or repair a file means knowing where on the hard disk it should be and where on the Windows CD you can find it. The error message should specify the hard disk location of the damaged file but it is by no means easy to discover where to find the replacement on the CD. This is because the files are compressed to save space and hidden in 'cabinets'. A cabinet is like a Zip file with a .CAB extension and it isn't easy to locate the compressed files within one. Do a web search for the file you want, remembering that each edition of Windows has its own set of CAB files.

Here is a worked example. Say, for example, you are using Windows 98 SE and you need to replace a file called *ios.vxd*. An error message tells you that the file belongs in the *C:\Windows\System\VMM32* folder. If you search the Microsoft Knowledge Base for keywords "*ios.vxd cabinet 98*", you will learn that the file is stored in the *Win98_54.cab* file on the Windows 98 CD-ROM (all the Windows 98 SE cabinet files are in a folder on the CD called *Win98*).

Here is how to replace a damaged file with a fresh version from a CD:

Start your computer with a Windows start-up floppy disk. If necessary, change the BIOS to boot from the floppy drive first (see Appendix 1). Select the CD-ROM support option.

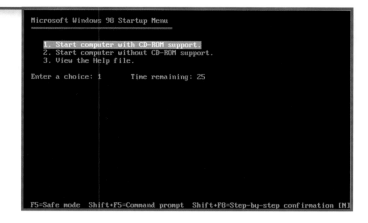

```
Microsoft Windows 98 Startup Menu


1. Start computer with CD-ROM support.
2. Start computer without CD-ROM support.
3. View the Help file.

Enter a choice: 1        Time remaining: 25




F5=Safe mode  Shift+F5=Command prompt  Shift+F8=Step-by-step confirmation [N]
```

Insert the Windows 98 installation CD-ROM in its drive and note the drive letter assigned to that drive (probably D: or, as shown, here, E:).

```
Preparing to start your computer.
This may take a few minutes. Please wait...

The diagnostic tools were successfully loaded to drive D.

MSCDEX Version 2.25
Copyright (C) Microsoft Corp. 1986-1995. All rights reserved.
        Drive E: = Driver MSCD001 unit 0

To get help, type HELP and press ENTER.

A:\>
```

    C:

    Press the Enter key

    cd\windows\system\vmm32

    Press the Enter key

    extract e:\win98\win98_54.cab ios.vxd

    Press the Enter key

This rather convoluted procedure first sets the destination folder (Windows\System\VMM32) on the hard drive then extracts the target file (ios.vxd) from the cabinet file on the CD-ROM and copies it to the destination folder. Be sure to use the correct drive letter if it is anything other than E:. Also note the essential-but-easy-to-miss space between the name of the cab file and the name of the file you want to extract (in this case between Win98_54.cab and ios.vxd).

```
Preparing to start your computer.
This may take a few minutes. Please wait...

The diagnostic tools were successfully loaded to drive D.

MSCDEX Version 2.25
Copyright (C) Microsoft Corp. 1986-1995. All rights reserved.
        Drive E: = Driver MSCD001 unit 0

To get help, type HELP and press ENTER.

A:\>c:

C:\>CD \WINDOWS\SYSTEM\VMM32

C:\WINDOWS\SYSTEM\VMM32>EXTRACT E:\WIN98\WIN98_54.CAB IOS.VXD
Microsoft (R) Cabinet Extraction Tool - Version (16) 1.00.603.0 (08/14/97)
Copyright (c) Microsoft Corp 1994-1997. All rights reserved.

 Cabinet WIN98_54.CAB

Overwrite ios.vxd (Yes/No/All)?
```

4

 y

Press the Enter key

When asked to confirm the overwriting of ios.vxd, press Y for Yes and then hit the Enter key. Now remove the CD-ROM and floppy disk and restart your computer.

```
Overwrite ios.vxd (Yes/No/All)?Y
Extracting ios.vxd

C:\WINDOWS\SYSTEM\VMM32>_
```

There must be an easier way

It is no fun trying to coax a non-booting Windows system into action. You can find yourself replacing one damaged file after another for hours on end without getting anywhere, so it is nearly always easier to reinstall Windows from a backup or image file if you have one (see p18).

Trying to fix Windows by reinstalling a good version on top of a bad one is not a good idea. It seldom works as well as you hope and often causes problems by overwriting updated versions of programs with older ones. Internet connections and e-mail settings are particularly difficult to preserve. Ultimately, we think a clean install of Windows is preferable to a bodged repair.

Of course, you do have to back up your data first – which rather hammers home the importance of making frequent backups lest your computer should suddenly refuse to start and make this impossible – and you will need to reinstall all your programs as well as Windows itself. However, you will have the equivalent of a new computer at the end of it.

If your computer came with a custom-designed 'recovery' CD from the manufacturer, as is commonplace on new systems with Windows XP pre-installed, this is an even better option than manually installing Windows. Again, you should back up your data first because the recovery CD will replace everything that is on the hard disk, but you will end up with a freshly-installed version of Windows and all the bundled software just as it was on the day you first used the machine. Bear in mind that you will have to reload any software that you purchased subsequently and reconfigure customisations and personal settings (including your internet connection).

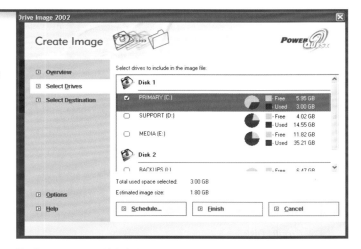

Backups are essential, but as Windows 2000 and XP Pro are the only two Microsoft products with a backup program worthy of the name, the rest of us need something like Norton Ghost or PowerQuest Drive Image (shown here) for peace of mind.

Windows will not close!

If your computer starts just fine but hangs whenever you try to shut it down, you are not alone. It is by no means as serious or debilitating as a start-up failure, but irritating nevertheless.

For help, look here:

- Windows 98 users: Microsoft Knowledge Base article no. 202633

- Windows Me users: Microsoft Knowledge Base article no. 273746

- Windows 98 Second Edition (SE) users: download the shutdown supplement from this web page:
  www.microsoft.com/windows98/downloads/contents/WUReco mmended/S_WUFeatured/Win98SE/Default.asp

- Windows XP users: **http://aumha.org/win5/a/shtdwnxp.htm**

This problem is relatively rare on Windows Vista, which has been redesigned to prevent misbehaving programs from delaying or preventing a system shutdown. You'll often find that a slow shutdown is caused by Windows installing essential system updates (it will tell you on screen if it's doing this). If that isn't the culprit, head for the Windows Vista Solutions Centre at **http://support.microsoft.com/ph/11732**.

Another possible cause – on all versions of Windows – is that your PC has become infected with a virus or similar nasty. Run a full virus scan and, on Windows 2000, XP or Vista, try the Windows Malicious Software Removal Tool. It's a free download from **www.microsoft.com/security/malwareremove/default.mspx**.

Making a Windows start-up disk

Have a blank floppy disk handy. In Windows 98 or Windows Me:

 Start

 Settings

 Control Panel

 Add/Remove Programs

On the Start-up Disk tab:

 Create Disk

Follow the on-screen instructions.

To make a start-up disk in Windows XP:

 Start

 My Computer

 Drive A:

 Format from the context menu

In the Format dialogue box, place a tick next to Create an MS-DOS Start-up Disk, and then click Start. Follow the on-screen instructions. Note, however, that an XP start-up disk only gets you to a DOS prompt; it contains no utilities or diagnostic tools

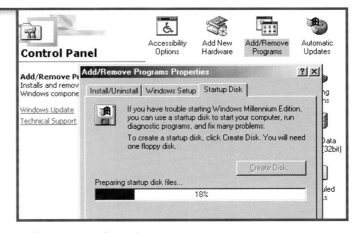

Making a start-up floppy in Windows Me.

and is thus of very limited use. The Recovery Console is the way to go here.

The Windows 2000 equivalent to a start-up disk is an Emergency Repair disk made within its Backup program.

You don't need to make a boot disk for Windows Vista, because the installation DVD is also a boot disk. It includes Startup Repair, which can fix many problems that prevent Windows from loading (see p32).

TROUBLESHOOTING

Safe Mode troubleshooting

Safe Mode is a state of reduced functionality that Windows voluntarily reverts to when it would otherwise be unable to run correctly. Only the essential parts of Windows are loaded in Safe Mode, so if a problem has been caused by a missing, damaged or unsuitable file, Windows is able to start safely by ignoring it.

Another situation in which Safe Mode saves the day is when you have added new hardware that competes with existing components for the attention of Windows. In its role as traffic manager, Windows needs to be able to set up clear channels of communication for each component in the system. It must also allocate a fair share of the computer's total resources to each component. If it is unable to do this during the boot sequence, then by switching to Safe Mode it avoids the inconvenience of starting up (apparently) normally but with a time-bomb ticking away in the background.

```
Microsoft Windows Millennium Startup Menu
==========================================

    1. Normal
    2. Logged (\BOOTLOG.TXT)
    3. Safe mode
    4. Step-by-step confirmation

Enter a choice: 3        Time remaining: 27

Warning: Windows did not finish loading on the previous attempt.
Choose Safe mode, to start Windows with a minimal set of drivers.
```

When Windows automatically enters Safe Mode, it reports only that it was unable to load on the previous attempt. The nature of the problem is not disclosed.

Situations that are likely to lead to Windows automatically entering Safe Mode are newly-added programs that conflict with the existing ones, hard disk errors, deleted system files, changed drivers, and attempting to remove a program without using the Add/Remove Programs option in Windows Control Panel. Often, you can get away with drastic acts of computer savagery while Windows is running, but when you try to restart and Windows has to load all its system files again, it is forced into Safe Mode for its own protection.

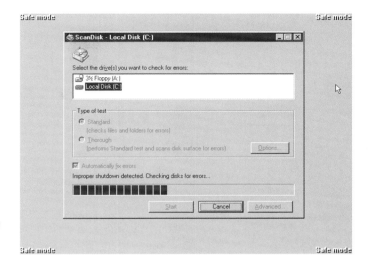

Windows always runs an automated disk check if entry into Safe Mode was caused by an improper shutdown of the previous session.

Forcing start-up in Safe Mode

There may be times when you wish to explicitly start Windows in Safe Mode, perhaps because your computer consistently crashes, freezes or throws up an error when running normally. Useful though Safe Mode is as an effective way of starting a shaky system, it is not a viable long-term solution because too many of the essential features of Windows are disabled.

To start in Safe Mode, press function key F8 as you switch on your computer. In Windows 98 and Me, hit the key just after the power-on messages about disk detection but before the Windows splash screen appears. In Windows XP, press F8 at any time after disk detection but before the loading band appears in the lower section of the screen. In Windows 2000, press F8 while the *Starting Windows* loading band is visible.

The advanced start-up options of Windows 2000.

You will eventually find yourself at an Advanced Options menu where you can choose how you want to start Windows. There are four start-up modes in Windows Me and six in Windows 98. Option 3 is Safe Mode. You might also find Option 4 (*Step-by-step confirmation*) useful. Think of it as a sort of customised Safe Mode in which you select which parts of Windows to load. For example, you might decide to skip the loading of the Windows Registry settings if you think a program you have recently installed has changed them for the worse. Or if you suspect a problem is being caused by a program or driver loaded by the two Windows start-up files (*autoexec.bat* and *config.sys*), you can step through these files a line at a time, accepting or rejecting each one in turn.

Windows XP and Windows 2000 present you with more start-up options than Windows 9x. For example there are three variations on Safe Mode: *with Networking*, *without Networking*, and the non-graphical *Command Prompt*. Unless you are familiar with command-driven operating systems such as MS-DOS and Linux, it is a good idea to avoid the Command Prompt mode unless under expert advice.

Two useful extra options are *Last Known Good Configuration* (the last settings that worked) and *Enable VGA mode*, which boots normally but in the simple VGA graphics mode, thus overcoming problems caused by damaged or incorrectly-set video drivers.

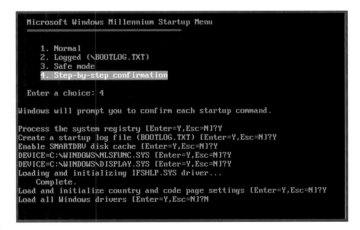

In this instance, Step-by-step confirmation is being used to load everything except Windows drivers.

What can I do in Safe Mode?

Here is a run-through of the main practical applications of using *Safe Mode*.

The very first thing to do after entering Safe Mode is to immediately close down Windows in the usual way from the Start button, then switch off your computer and wait for several seconds before switching it on again. It is amazing how often this does the trick.

If you have a virus checker, use it. You should be able to run it in Safe Mode from the hard disk. If not, use the emergency floppy created by all good anti-virus programs.

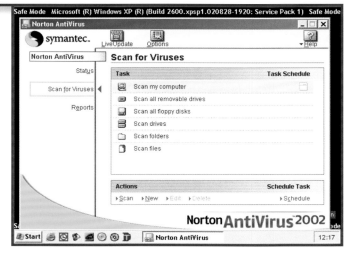

Although background virus protection will be disabled in Safe Mode, a manual virus scan can still be implemented.

When Safe Mode is launched in Windows Me, the first screen you see offers the services of a Safe Mode troubleshooter. Work through this before trying to track down the problem yourself. You may also manually invoke the troubleshooter from the Windows Help system.

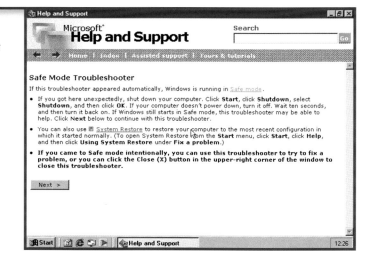

The Safe Mode troubleshooter is a feature only of Windows Me.

In Windows Me and Windows XP, the next logical step is to forget about troubleshooting altogether and simply use the System Restore tool to reinstate a system checkpoint from a time when you know Windows was working correctly. System Restore runs in Safe Mode just as it does after a normal Windows start-up. It can be invoked as an alternative to running the Safe Mode Troubleshooter in Windows Me or as an alternative to hands-on repairs in Windows XP:

 Start

 (All) Programs

 Accessories

 System Tools

 System Restore

If you don't have a suitable checkpoint (or if System Restore has been turned off on your machine), it might well be easier to reinstate Windows from a disk image backup rather than try to repair a damaged system manually (see p117). This is the only option for users of Window 98 or Windows 2000, neither of which has a System Restore feature.

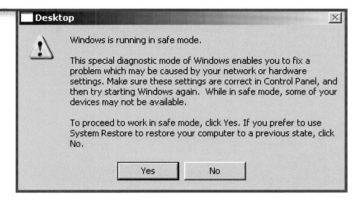

To run System Restore as an alternative to interactive Safe Mode in Windows XP, simply click No on the introductory screen.

If, prior to entering Safe Mode, you received an error message naming specific files as the cause of a problem, try reinstating them. There are many ways of doing this, the easiest being to reinstall the host program. However, if you can find the offending file on the source CD, you could simply copy it from there to the correct location on your hard disk, overwriting the faulty file in the process. This may or may not work. Other possibilities are reinstating the file from a conventional backup or extracting it from a hard disk image file created by a program like Norton Ghost or PowerQuest Drive Image (see p117). If you have access to the web you may also be able to download the file from there.

A disk image preserves every bit and byte of data on your computer and makes it easy to reinstate a corrupt or lost file.

The System Configuration Utility in Windows 98, Me and XP is an invaluable tool. To start it:

 Start

 Run

 msconfig

It gives you the power to selectively enable or disable many of the features of Windows and thereby discover by a process of elimination where the problem lies.

The Help menu within the System Configuration Utility advises you what to try first. This tool has become more sophisticated over the years so you will find a greater level of control in the Windows Me version than in Windows 98 and the most powerful set of options in Windows XP and Windows Vista. Incidentally, the Me, XP and Windows Vista versions include a file expander (look on the General tab) to extract compressed files from Windows installation CDs.

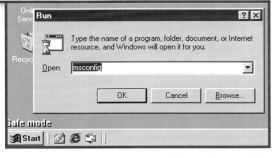

Starting the System Configuration Utility in Windows 98. It can also be accessed from the Start button using Start > Programs > Accessories > System Tools > System Information > System Configuration Utility.

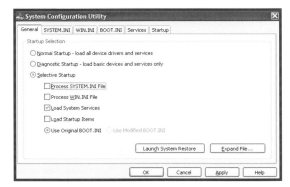

On the General tab in the System Configuration Utility, you choose which groups of files and services to process on start-up. With the other tabs you can enable or disable individual items. Search the Microsoft Knowledge Base for full details.

Before booting into Safe Mode, users of Windows XP, Windows 2000 and Windows Vista should try rebooting and selecting the Last Known Good Configuration option. This restores the Windows Registry to an earlier, hopefully working, version, which solves many ills at a stroke. With Windows 98 and Windows Me, you can also check and automatically restore the Registry with Registry Checker while in Safe Mode.

 Start

 Program

 Accessories

 System Tools

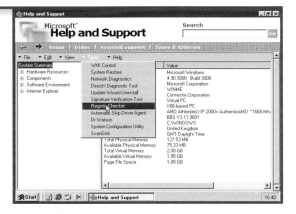 System Information

On the System Information Tools menu select Registry Checker and leave it to do its business

The Registry is Windows' record of hardware and software settings. But while choosing Last Known Good Configuration will use the previous working version, you will still have a problem if files mentioned in the Registry have been lost or damaged.

Registry Checker is available in Windows Me (shown here) and in Windows 98.

The Registry maintains a record of all that Windows needs to work. A problem here can have far-reaching consequences, which is why Windows makes regular backup copies.

While troubleshooting in Safe Mode, it is always worth checking the state of Device Manager, not only to discover potential hardware and driver problems but also to take the first steps towards eliminating them. To start Device Manager, open My Computer (the shortcut keystroke of Windows key + Pause is worth remembering). In Windows 9x, click the Device Manager tab. In Windows XP/2000, click the Hardware tab followed by the Device Manager button.

Devices marked with yellow exclamation points or red crosses are not working. The yellow marker indicates a problem; the red marker that the device has been disabled.

A communications port conflict, probably caused by using the wrong drivers while installing a modem (notice there is no modem in the hardware list).

In normal Windows mode, you can change the resources used by each device to resolve conflicts by trial and error, but this is impossible in Safe Mode because the drivers for the devices are not in use. What you can do is disable a device that is preventing Windows loading normally and forcing you into Safe Mode. This enables you to reboot into normal Windows mode and resolve the problem or reinstall the device and its driver. To disable a device, right-click its entry and select Properties. Select Do not use this Device (Windows XP/2000) or Disable in this Hardware Profile (Windows 98/Me).

Disable apparently troublesome hardware devices with Device Manager. If your computer now starts normally, you know where the problem lies.

 PART

How to use the Windows XP Recovery Console

Windows XP uses a slightly different file system to its predecessors, and this file system includes a number of automatic safeguards that do their best to prevent files from being damaged and which can repair files if they do get into trouble. That's why you don't get a bootable MS-DOS disk with Windows XP: it doesn't need one.

However, despite Microsoft's best efforts Windows XP is not absolutely secure. It can be affected by mechanical failure, sudden interruption of power, wilful or accidental damage, and viruses. And, like every operating system, it contains bugs that may take years to manifest themselves. That's why Windows XP still needs an MS-DOS-style emergency operating mode for those rare occasions when it cannot boot from its hard disk. This mode is called the Recovery Console, and in this chapter we'll discover how to launch it and use it to repair your copy of Windows.

Starting Recovery Console

All of the files needed to start Recovery Console are on the Windows XP CD-ROM but in order to use them you must first set your computer to boot from its CD-ROM drive. If your computer normally boots from its floppy or hard disk – many machines are pre-configured this way – you will need to make changes within the BIOS setup program to give priority to the CD drive (see Appendix 1). Once this has been done, place the Windows XP CD-ROM in the CD drive and restart your computer. The hard disk will now be bypassed and the computer will boot instead from the CD-ROM.

You are prompted to press any key to continue. After a short wait, you are presented with a blue Windows Setup screen offering three options: install Windows from scratch; repair the existing installation using Recovery Console; or quit without doing either. Press *R* to start Recovery Console.

You are asked to specify which installation of Windows you want to log on to, but this question only really applies if there is more than one version of Windows installed on your computer (i.e. you have a dual or multiple boot setup). For a standard Windows installation, type *1* to confirm the default location. When prompted, type in your administrator's password. If you normally operate without a password, just press Enter.

```
Microsoft Windows XP(TM) Recovery Console.

The Recovery Console provides system repair and recovery functionality.

Type EXIT to quit the Recovery Console and restart the computer.

1: C:\WINDOWS

Which Windows installation would you like to log onto
(To cancel, press ENTER)? ▪
```

If you decide NOT to run Recovery Console, remove the Windows CD-ROM and press F3.

```
Microsoft Windows XP(TM) Recovery Console.

The Recovery Console provides system repair and recovery functionality.

Type EXIT to quit the Recovery Console and restart the computer.

1: C:\WINDOWS

Which Windows installation would you like to log onto
(To cancel, press ENTER)? ▪
```

Your last chance to back out before entering Recovery Console mode.

Using Recovery Console

At this stage, you might think that nothing has happened because you are looking at an unresponsive, unhelpful text screen. But with Recovery Console this is as good as it gets. At the prompt, you can type commands to copy or replace operating system files and folders, to disable services or devices that may be preventing Windows from loading, or to repair a damaged disk. To list all the available commands, type *Help*. For help with a particular command, type the name of the command followed by a space and */h* e.g. *Delete /h*.

The use of Recovery Console should be regarded as a last resort. To get the best out of it you need expert help or a clear set of instructions relating to your problem, possibly downloaded and printed from the web on another computer. Without such support it is best to stick to straightforward disk and file maintenance.

Three easy-to-use commands are *Fixmbr* to rewrite the master boot record of drive 0 (in a normal computer this is where Windows resides); *Fixboot* to repair the boot sector of the default drive; and *Chkdsk* to perform a disk integrity check. If *Chkdsk* finds problems with the disk, run it again with a space and */r* after the command – i.e. *Chkdsk /r* – to attempt a repair.

To run Fixmbr, Fixboot or Chkdsk all you have to do is type the command name and press Enter.

Replacing damaged or missing files

When Windows fails to start, it either announces that it has run into a software or hardware problem, the nature of which is unspecified, or it helpfully identifies the files at the heart of the problem. In the latter case you can replace the guilty files with fresh versions from your Windows XP CD using the *Copy* and *Expand* commands within the Recovery Console. Copy is for ready-to-use files stored under their own names on the Windows XP CD. Expand is for compressed files stored in Microsoft's CAB format. It also works with individual compressed files that are stored under their own names but with the last letter of the file extension replaced by an underscore.

You need to know both the source folder of the target file on the CD-ROM and the hard disk folder to which it should be sent. The two files most likely to require reinstatement are the crucial boot files *Ntldr* and *NTdetect.com*. To replace them with uncompressed originals from the *i386* folder of a CD in drive D: you would issue the following sequence of commands at the command prompt within *Recovery Console*. Note that typed commands are case-insensitive:

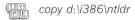 *cd ..*

This changes the active folder from *C:\Windows* to *C:*. Note that the *cd* command is followed by a space and two dots.

 copy d:\i386\ntldr

This copies the *Ntldr* file from the CD-ROM to the selected folder on the hard disk.

 y

This confirms that it is okay to overwrite the file currently on the hard disk with the file from the CD-ROM.

 copy d:\i386\ntdetect.com

This now copies the *NTdetect.com* file from the CD-ROM to the hard disk.

 y

Again, overwrite confirmation is required.

 exit

This closes *Recovery Console*. Remove the Windows CD-ROM before the computer reboots.

Replacing two critical system files with the help of the Recovery Console.

Fixing Stop Errors

Blue screen stop errors may occur at any time, even, infuriatingly, while Windows is loading. When this happens, you cannot replace the offending file using Windows Explorer but you can replace it using Recovery Console.

Stop error *0x0000007B* is a typical example. When accompanied by the message *INACCESSIBLE BOOT DEVICE*, it indicates an incorrect set of drivers and Registry entries for the hard disk. Article Q314082 in the Microsoft Knowledge Base provides the information that four drivers need to be extracted from the *Driver.cab* file in the *i386* folder on the Windows CD-ROM and placed in the *Windows\System32\Drivers* folder on the hard disk. One of these files is called *Pciide.sys*. As a pattern for similar activities, here is how to extract it to the correct location.

Start Recovery Console and ensure that the Windows XP CD-ROM is in the drive (which has the drive letter D: in this example).

 cd \windows\system32\drivers

This tells Windows to place all expanded files into this folder.

 expand d:\i386\driver.cab /f:pciide.sys

The */F:* part of the command specifies the name of the single file within *Driver.cab* that you wish to target.

 exit

Once the file is copied, remove the CD-ROM and type Exit to reboot your computer.

```
C:\WINDOWS>cd \windows\system32\drivers

C:\WINDOWS\SYSTEM32\DRIVERS>expand D:\i386\Driver.cab /F:pciide.sys
pciide.sys
          1 file(s) expanded.

C:\WINDOWS\SYSTEM32\DRIVERS>_
```

It is notoriously difficult to get long commands right the first time you type them. If you receive an error message, press Enter and try again on a new line.

Repairing the installation

If a repair attempt using Recovery Console is unsuccessful, you might decide to reinstall Windows. This can either be a full installation, which also means reinstalling third-party programs and reinstating your personal files from a backup, or you can try a repair installation that keeps your current programs, settings and data. Be aware that after a repair installation you must reapply any Windows upgrades and service packs and also reactivate Windows XP online.

To start a repair installation, boot from the Windows XP CD-ROM as described above but do not press *R* for Recovery Console. Instead, press *Enter*. On the next screen, press *F8* to agree to the licence arrangements; and on the screen after that, press *R* to perform a repair installation. During the repair, ignore any messages about rebooting from the CD and let Setup continue as if doing a fresh install.

A repair installation doesn't always do the trick but it is worth a try, especially if you have a complicated Windows system involving many third-party programs, passwords and customised settings. A full installation always works provided the hardware inside your computer is in good order.

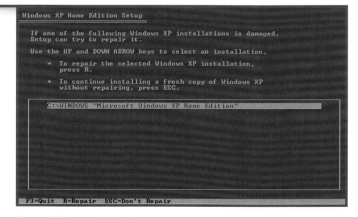

If your PC has multiple Windows installations (only one is available here), select the correct one before pressing R to repair. There's no going back afterwards.

Obtaining Windows XP setup disks

It isn't always possible to configure certain older computers to boot from their CD-ROM drives, which makes it impossible to start Recovery Console in the usual way. The solution is to obtain Windows XP setup disks by downloading them from Microsoft's support website. You can then boot your computer from a floppy disk and gain access to the CD-ROM drive.

Use this URL to access Microsoft's download page: **http://support.microsoft.com/default.aspx?scid=KB;en-us;q310994**. There are different downloads for Windows XP Home and Professional versions, for foreign languages, and for computers with SP1 installed, so make sure you get the right one.

The download is a single program file but when you run it a set of six floppies will be created. Have sufficient spare disks handy.

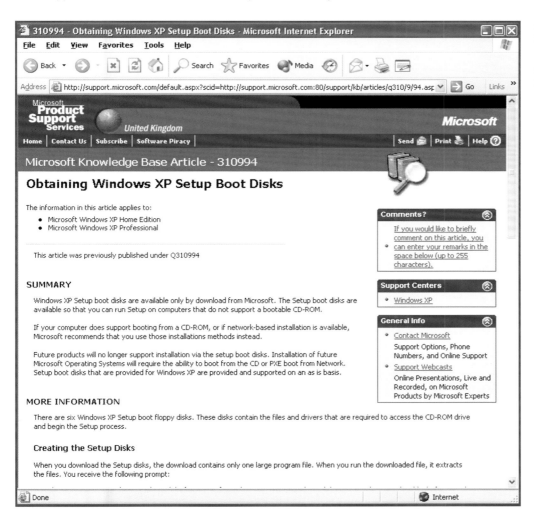

Microsoft has already announced that no future versions of Windows will be bootable from floppies, so this website marks the end of an era.

TROUBLESHOOTING

Recovery options in Windows Vista

Windows Vista doesn't have a Recovery Console. Instead, it has a number of tools on the installation disc. To access the tools, you'll need to launch the System Recovery Options menu. To do this:

1. Insert the Windows Vista installation disc.
2. Restart your computer.

 Choose your language settings and then click on Next

 Click Repair Your Computer

 Select your operating system and then click on Next

Depending on the version of Windows Vista you have, you should now see some or all of the following options:

Startup Repair
This option fixes common problems, such as missing or damaged files, that prevent Windows from starting properly.

System Restore
Unless you've disabled the System Restore function in Windows Vista, which automatically takes 'snapshots' of your system in case of disaster, this option enables you to restore your computer to the last system restore point. This option restores system files and does not damage your personal files such as documents or digital photos.

Windows Complete PC Restore
This option is only available to users of Windows Vista Ultimate Edition or Business Edition. It enables you to restore your entire hard disk from a backup copy.

Windows Memory Diagnostic Tool
This tool scans your PC's memory to see if there are any problems. If Windows Vista is misbehaving after a memory upgrade, this is the tool you want to use.

Command Prompt
A direct replacement for the XP Recovery Console, the Command Prompt tool is really designed for advanced users. You'll find a full list of Command Prompt commands at:
**http://windowshelp.microsoft.com/Windows/en-US/Help/
4e7cd306-e9b0-4296-9528-9121d4f9bd111033.mspx**.

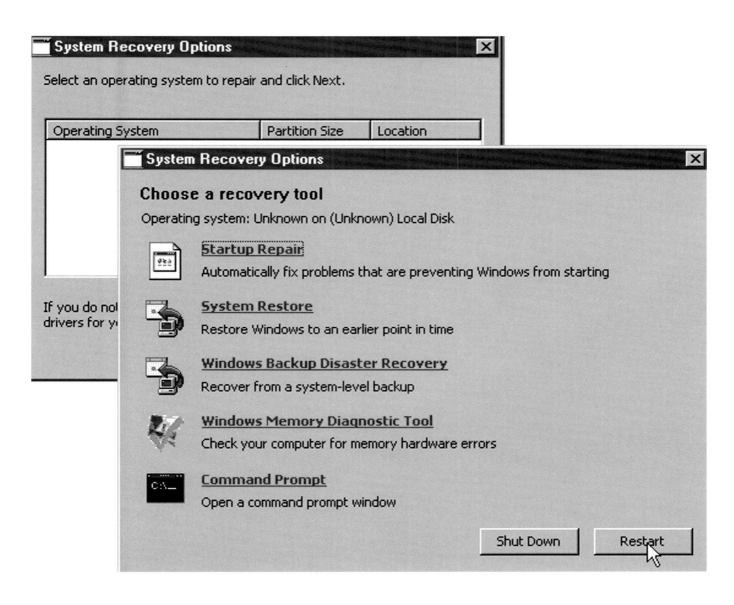

System Recovery Options

Select an operating system to repair and click Next.

Operating System	Partition Size	Location

If you do not
drivers for y

System Recovery Options

Choose a recovery tool

Operating system: Unknown on (Unknown) Local Disk

Startup Repair
Automatically fix problems that are preventing Windows from starting

System Restore
Restore Windows to an earlier point in time

Windows Backup Disaster Recovery
Recover from a system-level backup

Windows Memory Diagnostic Tool
Check your computer for memory hardware errors

Command Prompt
Open a command prompt window

Shut Down   Restart

Windows Vista has an extensive set of recovery tools. To use them, restart your PC with the installation disc in your CD or DVD drive, choose your language and then select Repair Your Computer.

Get Windows Vista to find and fix problems automatically

Windows Vista has a new feature, called the Problem Reports and Solutions Center. This can automatically check the internet for solutions to problems. For example, if a hardware driver isn't working it can often find an updated driver for you. To enable this feature, click on Start > Control Panel > System and Maintenance > Problem Reports and Solutions. In the left-hand panel, click on Change Settings and then click on Check For Solutions Automatically (recommended). Click on OK and Windows Vista will now attempt to heal itself when it encounters problems.

Dealing with DLLs

Windows comes with a massive set of dynamic link library (DLL) files containing instructions and routines that can be drawn upon by Windows and by any other program that needs to use the same resources. Because of the shared nature of DLL files, any problems with them can create knock-on effects with system-wide consequences.

The main problem with a DLL is not that it suffers damage or is inadvertently deleted, but that it is replaced by an out-of-date version. The original Microsoft DLL files (supplied on Windows CD-ROMs and with other Microsoft programs) may be overwritten by older, but still genuine, Microsoft files with the same name. The substitute files may be delivered with software from Microsoft itself or from third-party software providers; the longer the software has been sitting on your shelf, the more likely it is to include potentially troublesome out-of-date files.

Microsoft's DLL files are always backwards-compatible with earlier files of the same type and with the same name, which means that the new version of a DLL file won't only do everything the old file did but may also incorporate additions and improvements. Unfortunately Microsoft doesn't subscribe to the idea of forward compatibility, so there is no guarantee that Windows will continue to work normally if you accidentally replace a new DLL with an older one that doesn't support the latest features.

isrt.dll	.dll	331,776	Application Extension	05/09/2001	04:20	C:\Documents and Settings\Kyle the Worker\Local Settings\Temp\{7A900EAB-
isrt.dll	.dll	331,776	Application Extension	05/09/2001	04:20	C:\Documents and Settings\Kyle the Worker\Local Settings\Temp\{98172D29-
isrt.dll	.dll	331,776	Application Extension	05/09/2001	04:20	C:\Documents and Settings\Kyle the Worker\Local Settings\Temp\{B5BAAFAE-
isrt.dll	.dll	331,776	Application Extension	05/09/2001	04:20	C:\Documents and Settings\Kyle the Worker\Local Settings\Temp\{C6866B7D-
mfc42.dll	.dll	995,383	Application Extension	26/07/2000	17:00	C:\Documents and Settings\Kyle the Worker\Local Settings\Temp_ISTMP1.DII
mfc42.dll	.dll	995,383	Application Extension	26/07/2000	17:00	C:\Documents and Settings\Kyle the Worker\Local Settings\Temp_ISTMP2.DII
msvcp60.dll	.dll	401,462	Application Extension	29/08/2000	00:00	C:\Documents and Settings\Kyle the Worker\Local Settings\Temp_ISTMP1.DII
msvcp60.dll	.dll	401,462	Application Extension	29/08/2000	00:00	C:\Documents and Settings\Kyle the Worker\Local Settings\Temp_ISTMP2.DII
PlaceBar Customizer (MSOU...	.dll	172,808	Application Extension	24/12/2002	20:52	C:\Documents and Settings\Kyle the Worker\Application Data\Microsoft\AddIn
Sfpshlex.dll	.DLL	57,344	Application Extension	01/09/1999	22:54	C:\Documents and Settings\All Users\Documents\SFPack\
Shfolder.dll	.DLL	23,312	Application Extension	23/07/2001	00:00	C:\Documents and Settings\Kyle the Worker\Local Settings\Temp\CRF000\PCe
Shfolder.dll	.DLL	23,312	Application Extension	23/07/2001	00:00	C:\Documents and Settings\Kyle the Worker\Local Settings\Temp\CRF001\PCe
SrcSep.dll	.dll	110,592	Application Extension	08/09/1999	07:59	C:\Documents and Settings\Kyle the Worker\Local Settings\Temp\CRF000\PCe
SrcSep.dll	.dll	110,592	Application Extension	08/09/1999	07:59	C:\Documents and Settings\Kyle the Worker\Local Settings\Temp\CRF001\PCe
Uninstal.dll	.dll	148,992	Application Extension	24/12/2002	20:52	C:\Documents and Settings\Kyle the Worker\Application Data\Microsoft\AddIn
VPCKeyboard.dll	.dll	21,504	Application Extension	02/09/2003	11:41	C:\Documents and Settings\Kyle the Worker\Application Data\Connectix\Virtua

Your computer contains hundreds or even thousands of tiny but critical DLL files.

Diagnosing DLL problems

There are two ways you might discover that a DLL file needs replacing. One is when Windows delivers an error message naming a DLL file (this might be an internal Windows error from which a recovery is possible or a stop error that prevents Windows from loading); and the other is when Windows develops a fault and you track down the cause yourself using Microsoft or third-party websites describing known problems and solutions relating to DLLs.

If a Windows error message makes you suspect a DLL, you shouldn't replace it without further investigation, because error messages don't always point to the root of the problem. Always conduct a web search to see if there is a tried-and-tested solution to your problem. If you decide to go ahead and replace a DLL anyway, you can do no harm as long as you are scrupulous about checking the DLL file you intend to use as a replacement against the recommendations of the DLL Help Database.

After receiving the Windows error message Apr.exe is linked to missing Export Mfc42.dll, *a Google search on the words* Missing Mfc42.dll *reveals that* Mfc42.dll *is a known troublemaker.*

The DLL help database

DLL problems are less likely to plague you if you have a more recent version of Windows that incorporates digital 'signing' of files. This file protection feature was introduced in Windows Me to prevent critical system files from being replaced by non-working versions and it has been strengthened in Windows XP/2000. Nevertheless, you might still encounter problems with third-party programs if they were written to work with only one version of a DLL. Although this is bad programming technique, it is fairly common practice.

Windows 98 and, to a lesser extent, Windows Me are the versions of Windows most likely to suffer from problems caused by mix-and-match DLLs. Anybody running either of these operating systems should add Microsoft's DLL Help Database to their list of web favourites (type *DLL Help Database* into Google and use the *I'm Feeling Lucky* button to go straight there).

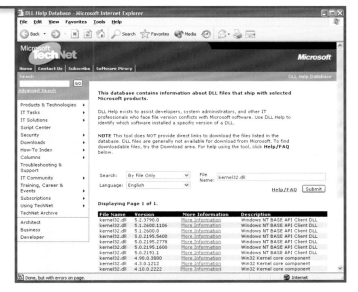

With so many versions of Kernel32.dll to choose from there is plenty of room for confusion. Click More Information *to find the one you need.*

By searching the database, you can check your copy of a DLL against the official version to see if they match.

Make a note of the correct DLL version number as listed in the database and then find out which version you are currently using by starting Windows Explorer and browsing to the folder on the hard disk where the DLL is located.

If you don't know the whereabouts of a DLL, use the Find function (Windows 98) or Search function (Windows Me) on the Start menu. Once you have located the file, right-click on it, select Properties from the context menu and then click the Version tab. If there is a discrepancy, the DLL Help Database will tell you where on your Windows CD-ROM you can find the replacement.

This version of Hotplug.dll (5.1.2600.0) is correct for Windows XP Home and Professional.

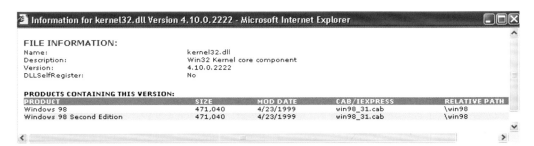

After requesting More Information in the DLL Help Database, you are told which version of Windows a file is for and where to find it on the CD-ROM.

Replacing a DLL using Windows

If a DLL you wish to replace isn't already in use, there is nothing to stop you replacing it using the file management tools built into Windows. The Microsoft-approved method of replacing files with originals extracted from CAB files is to use either System File Checker (Windows 98 only) or System Configuration Utility (Windows Me and XP).

However, if a DLL is processed automatically during start-up and Windows is already using it, replacing it from within Windows would be a recipe for disaster. From Windows Me onwards, such files are subject to a built-in system of file protection and their replacement is forbidden. The solution for Windows XP/2000 users is to replace the file using Recovery Console. The Windows 98/Me equivalent is to boot from a start-up floppy and use the Extract command, exactly as you would in a situation when Windows won't start at all.

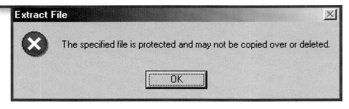

You cannot replace protected system files while Windows Me is running.

To start System File Checker in Windows 98:

 Start

 Run

 SFC

 OK

Select the option *Extract one file from installation disk* and either type in its name or use the Browse button to navigate to a saved file if you have recently downloaded a fresh copy. Click Start. Now, in the *Restore from* panel, type *D:\Win98* (assuming that D: is the CD-ROM drive). In the *Save File in* panel, type *C:\Windows\System* (or whatever happens to be the correct location). Finally, click *OK* and let Windows do the rest. Note that you don't need to know which CAB file the DLL is stored in.

To start System Configuration Utility in Windows Me or XP:

 Start

 Run

 msconfig

 OK

When you click the Extract button in Windows Me, you are presented with identical options to those described for Windows 98. The only difference is that in Windows Me the CAB files are in *D:\Win9x* rather than *D:\Win98*.

Windows XP works slightly differently. After starting the System Configuration Utility, click the Expand File button and enter the name of the file to be restored (just as you would in Windows 98/Me). However, in the *Restore from* panel you must enter the name of the correct CAB file as well as the CD-ROM folder where it resides.

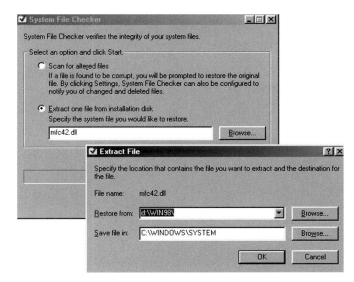

System File Checker in action in Windows 98.

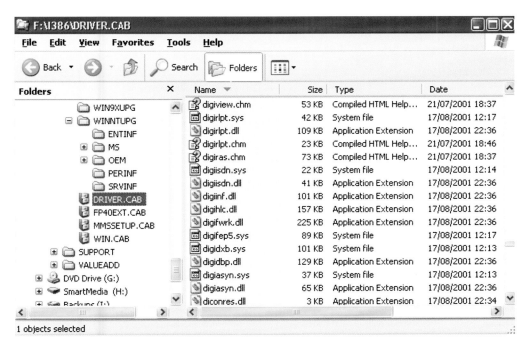

The contents of the Driver.cab *file on the Windows XP CD-ROM. Files dragged from the CAB file in* Windows Explorer *and dropped onto the hard disk are automatically extracted.*

You can glean this information from the DLL Help Database. The CAB files are in the *i386* folder so your *Restore from* entry will be something like *D:\i386\Drivers.cab*. The most likely destination is *C:\Windows\System32* but you may specify any other folder.

The only effective way of replacing DLL files in Windows 2000 is with the Recovery Console.

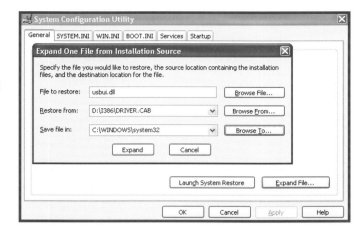

DLL replacement in Windows XP using the System Configuration Utility.

Replacing a DLL using MS-DOS

If Windows XP or 2000 won't start, you can expand files from the Windows CD-ROM using Recovery Console (see p28). However, there is no such facility in Windows 98 or Windows Me. The solution is to perform the repairs in MS-DOS mode by using a start-up floppy disk and typing in the appropriate commands.

When booting from a start-up floppy it is essential to choose CD-ROM support if you need to extract replacement DLLs.

As a pattern for all such replacements, here is how to replace Kernel32.dll, a key system file which, if damaged, prevents Windows from starting. The example assumes the Windows 98 CD-ROM is in drive E: and that we know from the DLL Help Database that Kernel32.dll is located in the cabinet file *Win98\Win98_31.cab*. It needs to be extracted to the *C:\Windows\System* folder on the hard disk.

Boot from the start-up floppy (selecting CD-ROM support) and note the identifying letter of the CD-ROM drive. Insert the Windows CD-ROM and type the following commands:

 c:

 Press the Enter key

This switches from floppy disk *A:* to hard disk *C:*.

 cd windows\system

 Press the Enter key

This switches to the destination folder.

 extract e:\win98\win98_31.cab kernel32.dll

 Y

This extracts the target file from the CD-ROM and copies it to the destination folder on the hard disk. Finally, remove the floppy disk and reboot your computer.

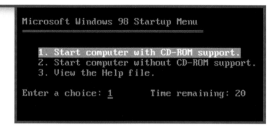

Extracting a replacement Kernel32.dll *file from the* Windows 98 CD-ROM.

In Windows Me the procedure is identical except that the extraction command must reflect the different location of the CAB files on the Windows Me CD-ROM i.e., in this case, the command would be '*extract e:\win9x\win_11.cab kernel32.dll*'.

When replacing a DLL, be sure to confirm the overwriting of the original.

No Windows CD-ROM?

Microsoft doesn't make DLLs available through its DLL Help Database. To do so might encourage the sort of mix-and-match file problem that the site is designed to tackle. However, there may be times when the correct CD-ROM isn't readily available and on such occasions you can turn to a number of websites where individual DLL files can be downloaded. We support Microsoft's point of view that making DLLs freely available is likely to cause as many problems as it solves, but if you desperately need to download a file, use a service such as the one provided at **www.dll-files.com.** You can view the version number of a file without having to download it first.

Need a DLL? One of the more reliable sources is www.dll-files.com.

TROUBLESHOOTING

Windows in-built troubleshooting toolkit

In computing circles, a tool isn't necessarily something you hold in your hand and a toolkit isn't kept in a car. Software tools are utility programs designed to help you diagnose and fix problems in other programs and there are plenty of tools to choose from. But why waste money when most of what you need is built into Windows? These tools are sometimes tucked away in the less accessible corners of Windows but with the help of this alphabetically-arranged guide, you will soon root them out.

Some of these utilities are purely diagnostic, others can be used for repair and recovery, and the third group consists of maintenance tools designed to keep problems at bay. As with all tools, it makes sense to learn how to use them before you need them rather than when disaster strikes.

No need for a screwdriver in a software toolkit.

Backup

Purpose: Recovery

Description: A means of copying entire hard disks or selected folders and files onto another form of media (usually removable disks or tapes) so that Windows can be restored if it bites the dust. The reinstatement of individual files is also possible.

Available in: 98, Me, XP, 2000, Vista

Where to find it: Backup is installed by default in Windows 2000, Windows XP Professional and Windows Vista.

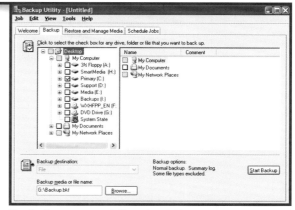

The Backup program delivered with Windows XP Home was designed for use with XP Pro. Most of the functions are also available in XP Home, but not the facility to reinstate Windows from a command prompt.

In Windows 2000 and XP:

 Start

 All Programs

 Accessories

 System Tools

In Windows Vista:

 Start

 Control Panel

 System and Maintenance

 Backup and Restore Center

If you have the Home Basic version of Windows Vista, you get a very basic backup utility, but in Home Premium and Ultimate editions you can get Windows Vista to run backups automatically at specific times.

In other versions of Windows, it is an optional component. To install Backup in Windows 98, open Control Panel and double-click Add/Remove programs. Then click the Windows Setup tab, double-click System Tools and place a check against Backup.

Users of Windows Me will find Backup on the CD-ROM in the *Addons\Msbackup* folder. Double-click *MSBEXP.EXE* to install it.

In Windows XP Home edition, Backup is on the CD-ROM in a folder called *Valueadd\MSFT\ntbackup*. Double-click the executable file named *NTBACKUP.MSI*.

Device Manager

Purpose: Diagnosis/Repair

Description: Device Manager displays the hardware components of a computer and indicates the drivers and other system resources that they depend on. Conflicts are easily found because they are flagged by markers. Resources can be reallocated and drivers changed if necessary.

Available in: 98, Me, XP, 2000, Vista

Where to find it: There are many shortcuts to Device Manager but here are the full routes from the Start button.

Device Manager in Windows XP has a Roll Back Driver facility to revert a problem driver to an earlier (working) version.

In Windows 98/Me:

 Start

 Settings

 Control Panel

 System

 Device Manager

In Windows XP:

 Start

 Control Panel

 Performance and Maintenance

 System

 Hardware

 Device Manager

In Windows 2000:

 Start

 Settings

 Control Panel

 System

 Hardware

 Device Manager

In Windows Vista:

 Start

 Control Panel

 System and Maintenance

Device Manager

Disk Cleanup

Purpose: Maintenance

Description: Removes unnecessary, little-used and temporary files that are clogging up your hard disk.

Available in: 98, Me, XP, 2000, Vista

Where to find it:

 Start

 (All) Programs

 Accessories

 System Tools

 Disk Cleanup

When using Disk Cleanup, you may preview files to check their contents before deleting them.

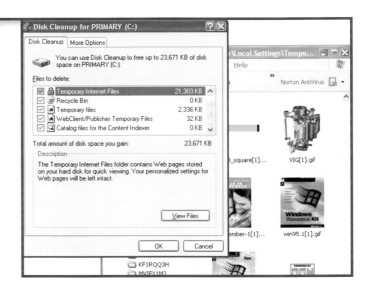

Disk Defragmenter

Purpose: Maintenance

Description: Organises a hard disk to minimise wasted space and consolidate large files which have become fragmented i.e. split apart and stored piecemeal all over the hard disk. The result is a marginal increase in disk access speed and a big increase in system stability.

Available in: 98, Me, XP, 2000, Vista

Where to find it:

 Start

 (All) Programs

 Accessories

 System Tools

 Disk Defragmenter

Disk Defragmenter can also be started from the Tools tab of a disk's Properties sheet if you right-click it in My Computer.

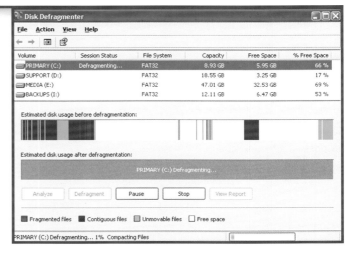

Windows Vista's Disk Defragmenter runs automatically, but you can start it manually by following the above steps.

Maintenance Wizard

Purpose: Maintenance

Description: Automates the operation of Disk Defragmenter, Disk Cleanup and ScanDisk

Available in: 98, Me

Where to find it:

 Start

 Programs

 Accessories

 System Tools

 Maintenance Wizard

Maintenance Wizard works in co-operation with the Scheduled Tasks utility. If you close Scheduled Tasks, the Maintenance Wizard won't operate.

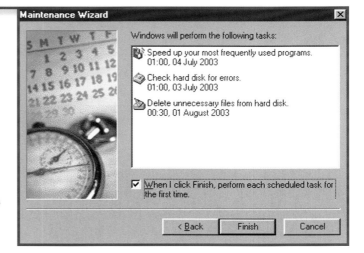

Registry Checker

Purpose: Diagnosis/Repair

Description: Checks the integrity of the Registry (the central store of system information in Windows). If Registry Checker finds faults, the Registry is replaced by one of five backup copies that are automatically maintained.

Available in: 98, Me

Where to find it:

 Start

 Programs

 Accessories

 System Tools

 System Information

On the *Tools* menu, click Registry Checker.

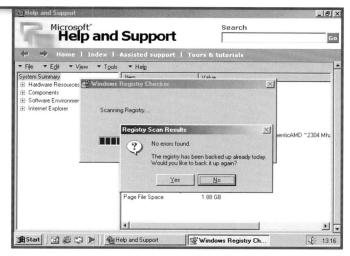

Registry Checker offers a convenient way of making an up-to-date backup of the Registry before attempting any major system changes.

ScanDisk

Purpose: Diagnosis/Repair

Description: Diagnoses and fixes many disk filing problems automatically. In its optional enhanced mode, it also checks the physical integrity of the disk surface. Though it may be able to restore a damaged filing system, it cannot repair individual files.

Available in: 98, Me, XP, 2000, Vista

Where to find it: In Windows 9x, use:

 Start

 Programs

 Accessories

 System Tools

 Scandisk

In Windows XP and 2000, open My Computer and right-click on the drive to be checked. From the *context* menu, select

 Properties

 Tools

 Check Now

In Windows Vista – you've guessed it – things are a little bit different. To scan your hard disk for errors, click Start > Computer and then right-click the hard disk drive you want to check for errors. Select Properties, click on the Tools tab, and under Error Checking click on Check Now.

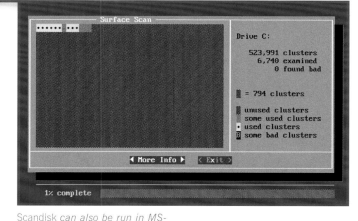

Scandisk can also be run in MS-DOS mode from the start-up floppy disks of Windows 98 and Windows Me.

System Configuration Utility

Purpose: Diagnosis/Repair

Description: Allows you to selectively enable or disable lines in several key Windows configuration files and to control which facilities and services are loaded. System Configuration Utility works in Safe Mode or after a conventional start-up.

Available in: 98, Me, XP, 2000, Vista

Where to find it:

 Start

 Run

 msconfig

 OK

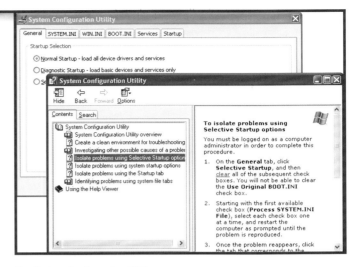

Once again, Windows Vista has moved things around. To launch the System Configuration Utility in Vista:

 Start

 Control Panel

 System and Maintenance

 Administrative Tools

 System Configuration

The System Configuration Utility Help menu offers detailed instructions on troubleshooting using selective start-up techniques.

System File Checker

Purpose: Diagnosis/Repair

Description: System File Checker keeps a log of all Windows system files and the changes made to them. If you suspect that a recently-installed program has overwritten or modified your Windows files you can check them and, optionally, reinstate the originals with this tool.

Available in: 98 only

Where to find it:

 Start

 Programs

 Accessories

 System Tools

 System Information

On the *Tools* menu,

 System File Checker

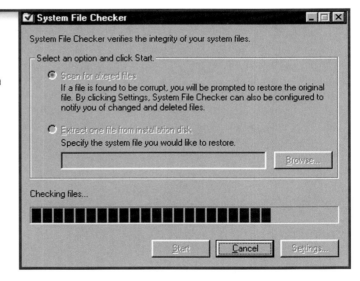

System File Checker was replaced in later versions of Windows by File Signature Verification (see the System Information tool).

System Information

Purpose: Diagnosis/Repair

Description: Probably the most powerful of all Windows tools. It does as its name suggests and delivers oceans of system information. Some of this is too arcane to be useful but it compensates by incorporating several invaluable utilities on the *Tools* menu. These vary according to the version of Windows you are running, but look out for Network diagnostics, DirectX diagnostics and the File Signature Verification tool that took the place of System File Checker.

Available in: 98, Me, XP, 2000

Where to find it:

 Start

 (All) Programs

 Accessories

 System Tools

System Information

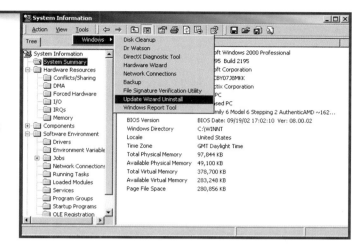

In Windows Me and 2000, the Tools menu of System Information includes something called Update Wizard Uninstall. This oddly-named but incredibly useful tool removes any Microsoft updates which may have adversely affected performance. Believe us, it happens.

System Monitor

Purpose: Diagnosis

Description: A program that runs in the background while you run other programs. It can be configured to display the workloads of processor, hard disk and memory and help you identify resource-hogging applications.

Windows XP and 2000 are equipped with much more sophisticated system monitoring tools in their Administrative Tools modules (accessible via Control Panel).

Available in: 98, Me

Where to find it: System Monitor is not installed by default. Install it via the Add/Remove Programs option in Control Panel (once there, look in the System Tools section of the Windows Setup tab). After installation, run System Monitor by:

 Start

 Programs

 Accessories

 System Tools

 System Monitor

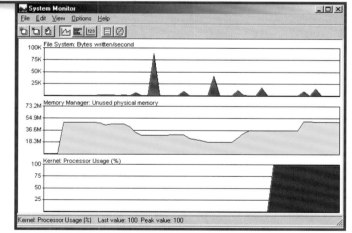

To change the information displayed by System Monitor, use the Add Item and Remove Item options on its Edit menu.

Task Manager

Purpose: Diagnosis/Recovery

Description: Task Manager is most often used to switch between programs but it is also useful as a means of ending a program which has stopped responding. In Windows XP and Windows 2000, it is also possible to use the Processes tab to terminate programs which do not show up on the Applications tab (e.g. anti-virus scanners that work permanently in the background or spyware).

Available in: 98, Me, XP, 2000, Vista

Where to find it: While holding down the CTRL and ALT keys, tap the DEL (Delete) key.

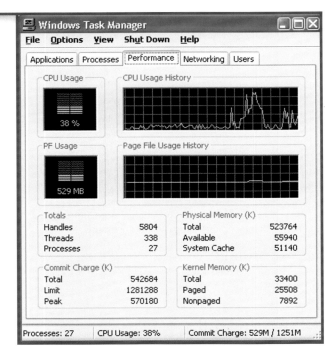

In Windows XP and 2000, the Performance tab of Task Manager provides a visual trace of the demands made on the processor and memory by recently-run programs.

Troubleshooting guides

Purpose: Diagnosis/Repair

Description: Step-by-step troubleshooting guides are built into the Windows Help system. Windows XP has the best selection in terms of quality and quantity, but in our experience the success rate when using troubleshooters is low unless you follow the instructions rigorously.

Available in: 98, Me, XP, 2000, Vista

Where to find them: In Windows 2000, click the Contents tab of the Windows Help system and go straight to the Troubleshooting and Maintenance section. In other versions of Windows, we suggest you type the word 'troubleshooter' into the Search or Find facility of Windows Help to get a longer list of 'hits'.

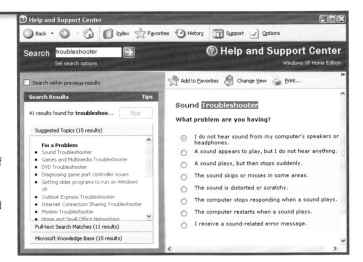

As well as the troubleshooters built into Windows XP, there are links to online troubleshooting resources in the Microsoft Knowledge Base.

Third-party troubleshooting software

Sisoftware SANDRA

One of the best diagnostic programs around is Sisoftware SANDRA from **www.sisoftware.co.uk.** There is a free downloadable standard product and a low-cost professional version. The Performance Tune-up Wizard analyses your PC and operating system, making recommendations for improvements where necessary.

System Mechanic

System Mechanic from **www.iolo.com** is also worth a look. It is free to use for 30 days and not only diagnoses problems but fixes them if it can.

Norton SystemWorks

If you're willing to pay for peace of mind, the market-leading program for home and office users is Norton SystemWorks from Symantec. As well as troubleshooting and maintenance tools, you get anti-virus protection and a copy of GoBack, a program that offers a souped-up system recovery feature similar to the one enjoyed by Windows Me and XP users. The program is not available for download but you can learn where to buy it at **www.symantec.com.**

Belarc Advisor

We also find the free Belarc Advisor utility invaluable when it comes to working out just what hardware and software components are installed on any given computer **(www.belarc.com/free_download.html)**. After a spot of analysis, it produces a detailed and comprehensive browser-based report.

SANDRA at work.

Suss out your system the easy way with Belarc.

Norton SystemWorks is a comprehensive utility suite.

Quick fixes for common problems

Not every Windows problem is a disaster in the making and there are quick fixes for many common glitches once you know what causes them. Some problems are not problems at all, but human errors – and sometimes not even that: they are the result of humans overestimating the intelligence of computers. We would not expect a person to be confused if we typed 'l' instead of '1' or zero instead of the letter 'O', but Windows will simply fail to find any file or program that is not spelled absolutely correctly. The people who send spam email messages know this, which is why they write V1AGRA instead of VIAGRA to fool the mail filters intended to block their messages.

In this section, we start with a few warnings about simple human errors that you can easily avoid. This is followed by a look at a larger group of errors, best described as Windows quirks. These are things you need to know about the way Windows works so you can help it keep on the straight and narrow. They are not serious problems that cause the permanent loss of data, but they are time-wasters that can be easily avoided once you know the secret.

Human errors

Problem: You try to copy a file onto a floppy disk and receive a message that the system cannot read from the specified device.
Solution: The floppy disk is write-protected, which isn't at all obvious from this Windows 98 description. To make it useable, slide the write protect tab away from the back edge of the disk and try again.

Problem: You try to restart Windows and receive this text message on a black background.
Solution: You have left a disk in the floppy disk drive. Remove it and press CTRL-ALT-DEL to reboot.

Problem: You try to delete a file from what you think is the hard disk and receive this error message.
Solution: You are inadvertently trying to delete a file from a CD-ROM. The Windows 98 message shown here is hopelessly misleading, but Windows XP recognises CD-ROMs for what they are and reminds you that you cannot delete files from them.

Problem: Everything you type looks strange. Letters you type with the Shift key held down appear in lower case, yet non-shifted letters are capitalised.

Solution: You have accidentally pressed the Caps Lock key. Using the Shift key when Caps Lock is on reverses its normal effect. This mistake is easy to spot if you are typing text into a word processor, but it can be a real puzzler if you are wondering why a password is not being accepted. Simply press Caps Lock again to correct the situation.

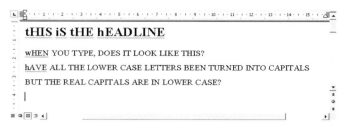

Windows quirks

Problem: You see a message that a file you are trying to move is in use by another program.

Solution: If the file you are trying to move really is in use by another program, simply switch to the other application and close the file. If the file is not currently in use, it may have been left hanging in a virtual limbo by an earlier program that closed unexpectedly. Reboot Windows and try again.

Problem: You try to delete or move a file in Windows 98 and receive a message citing *File error 1026.*

Solution: This very common error has more than one cause but the usual one is a lack of hard disk space (less than 100MB). You may also receive this error message while trying to save a file downloaded from the web, in which case the problem is too many files in the Temporary Internet Files folder. Free up some hard disk space with Disk Cleanup, archive seldom-needed files to removable storage media (like CD-R discs), or use a zip utility to compress large files.

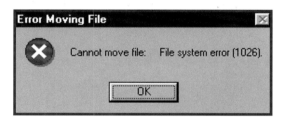

Problem: Windows cannot find a program and displays a message box headed *Missing Shortcut.*

Solution: The icons on the Start menu are merely shortcuts or links to where programs actually reside on the hard disk. If you move or delete a program, its shortcut ends up pointing at nothing and up pops an error message. Use the Browse button to show Windows where the program has been relocated or delete the superfluous shortcut.

Problem: Sound and video problems crop up in games and multimedia applications after installing new software.

Solution: Some elements of DirectX, the frequently updated multimedia component of Windows, may have been replaced by the new software. To put things right, download and install the latest version of DirectX from **www.microsoft.com.**

Problem: When you attempt to close Windows XP, it stops responding at the *Saving your settings* stage.
Solution: This is a known error in Windows XP and was fixed in Service Pack 1. If you do not wish to install Service Pack 1, you can obtain the patch separately through Windows Update, using procedures described in the Microsoft Knowledge Base article 307274. As a temporary fix, you can open Control Panel and click User Accounts > Change the way users log on or off. Remove the tick from Use the Welcome screen.

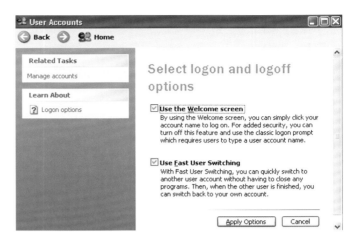

Problem: Windows XP or Windows Vista says you do not have permissions to make changes to Windows.
Solution: Unlike Windows 98 and Windows Me, only user accounts with administrative privileges can make system-wide changes in Windows XP and Windows Vista. Log on again using an administrator-level account.

Problem: Windows XP interrupts your work by dialling the internet to check for updates.
Solution: The automatic update feature in Windows is annoying unless you have an always-on internet connection. Turn it off using the Automatic Updates tab in the System Properties dialogue box (right-click My Computer and select Properties). You can initiate an update at any time with the Windows Update shortcut on the All Programs menu.

Problem: Desktop icons lose their colour for no apparent reason.
Solution: In Windows 98 and Windows Me, this happens when the option to show icons in all possible colours is selected but the colour depth is accidentally switched to 256 colours. Either increase the colour depth or disable the use of all possible colours on the Effects tab in Display Properties (right-click the Desktop to access Display Properties).

Problem: You change screen resolution and the screen image now flickers and seems less sharp than usual.
Solution: Even though you may have previously selected a suitable monitor refresh rate of 70Hz or higher, you will need to re-select it for each alternative resolution you choose.

 on the Desktop

 Properties

 Settings

 Advanced

 Monitor

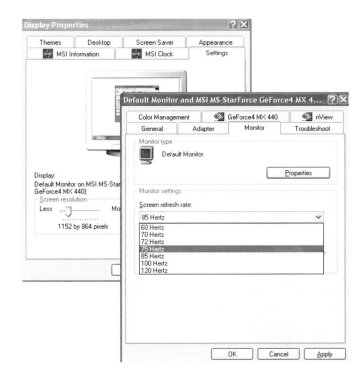

Problem: A program fails to start because a file beginning with the letters VB or MSVB is not found.
Solution: You are missing a required Visual Basic file. Visual Basic is a programming language that depends on a small number of so-called run-time files being present on the host machine. These files are not always supplied with the programs that need them, but you can download them from **http://support.microsoft.com/support/vbasic**. You don't need to reinstall the program as the error message implies.

Mapmaker.exe - Unable To Locate Component

This application has failed to start because VB40032.DLL was not found. Re-installing the application may fix this problem.

OK

Problem: You are warned that you are dangerously low on system resources and advised to quit any programs you are not using before your computer stops responding.
Solution: This is a common occurrence in Windows 98 and Windows Me, especially for people who use older software, but it can happen to anybody who uses a lot of programs at the same time. It indicates that the small amount of memory allocated to Windows for use as workspace is nearly full. You cannot fix the problem by adding more main memory, but you can fix the problem temporarily by closing down programs you no longer need. Better still, restart your computer to restore all the system resources to their default levels. An optional Windows system tool called Resource Meter can be installed from the Windows Setup tab of the Add/Remove Programs feature in the Control Panel.

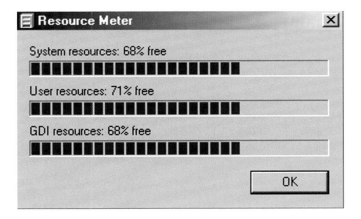

Web ways with Windows

The solution to almost every Windows problem you will ever encounter is on the web. With millions of Windows users around the world, you can safely bet that somebody, somewhere, has already had to deal with the problem that is now bugging you. If they have recorded their experiences online, as many do, all you have to do is find out where.

The first place to look for solutions to Windows problems is Microsoft's own support pages and in particular the Knowledge Base. Other sources are web forums and newsgroups where community-minded people help one another. There are also independent websites that offer expert help in response to user queries, although you do need to consider whether they are completely impartial or whether their ultimate aim is to sell you something; perhaps an anti-virus program, backup software or a paid subscription to a help service.

Microsoft's support site has a clever trick: when you start typing, it comes up with suggested searches. More often than not the suggestions include the exact thing you're looking for.

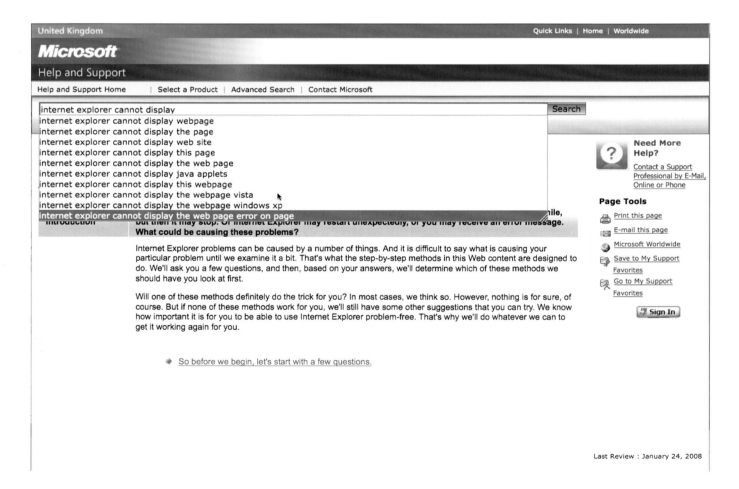

Introduction to the Microsoft Knowledge Base

The most powerful weapon in a problem-solving arsenal is a good search engine and there is none better (at the moment, anyway) than Google for general enquiries on troubleshooting topics. But Microsoft has its own search engine specifically geared to searching the company's extensive Knowledge Base collection of articles and FAQs (Frequently Asked Questions) covering Windows and all other Microsoft products.

The main Knowledge Base page is at **http://support.microsoft.com** and it is worth bookmarking this page. From here you can access five help areas:

- The Knowledge Base search engine

- Updates and patches for all products

- Personal assistance via e-mail or phone

- FAQs about specific products

- Microsoft community forums (newsgroups) covering specific products

Microsoft's support site should automatically redirect you to the correct country, but if it doesn't go to **www.microsoft.co.uk** *and then click on the Support link.*

Knowledge Base searching

If you need a solution to a Windows problem, the best place to start is with a search of the Knowledge Base. The wealth of information it contains is organised into articles, each of which has a unique ID number. If you know the number, you can type it straight into the Search box. Until December 2002, these article IDs were prefixed by letters (e.g. Q for the United States) but you can still use these older IDs if you type them without the letter.

Tracking down the answer to a problem when you don't have an article ID involves searching for words that clearly define the problem but don't produce too many false hits. It's no good typing something like *file not found* because you will get hundreds of results, so be sure to include the file's name too e.g. *Msvcrt.dll not found*.

It also helps if you change the search strategy from the default of *Any of the words entered* to *All of the words entered*. The first finds any article containing any of your search words (almost certainly too many to be of value), while the second finds only those articles containing all of your search words. With any luck, the one you need will be top of the list.

The Knowledge Base can be rather intimidating, so Microsoft has very helpfully provided links to the top troubleshooting issues to save you searching.

Tracking down error messages

If you are using the Knowledge Base to find an explanation for an on-screen error message, type the exact text of the error message and change the search strategy to *The exact phrase entered*.

Here is an example generated when running the Encarta Encyclopaedia: *Enc2000 caused a general protection fault in module dibeng.dll*. Searching for an exact match for this phrase in Knowledge Base delivers a single result explaining that the fault lies with the computer's ATI video card and not with Windows. The next step is to visit **www.ati.com** and download updated drivers.

Windows Update's error messages are wonderfully obscure but, if you take a note of the error number, Microsoft Support will tell you exactly what the problem is.

If the error message you are researching is a stop error (the so-called blue screen of death) in Windows 2000 or XP, then there is too much information for you to type it all in. All you need to know is that the line defining the error always begins with the word *STOP*, followed by five groups of numbers. On another line will be a term containing words separated by underscores, such as *IRQL_NOT_LESS_OR_EQUAL* or *FAT_FILE_SYSTEM*.

These are the key lines of a stop error screen. You can ignore the rest.

```
*** STOP: 0x00000023 (0x00000000,0x00000002,0x00000000,0x8038c240)
FAT_FILE_SYSTEM
```

To find the cause of the error, search for the first group of numbers shown after the word *STOP*. If this produces too many hits, narrow the search by also entering the descriptive term for the error, complete with its underscores. Because some stop errors affect only a single version of Windows, a search will be far more effective if you specify the version of Windows you are using in the *Select a Microsoft Product* section of the Search screen.

Click on Advanced Search to narrow your search criteria to specific products or to search not just Microsoft Support but the entire internet.

Newsgroups

The forums (newsgroups) accessible through Microsoft's support site can also be viewed using Outlook Express or any other newsgroup reader. All you have to do is type *microsoft.public.win* into your news reader and select from a list of 300 specialised groups.

The web-based browser for Microsoft's forums doesn't offer the features of a good newsreader but it does conveniently list groups by topic.

Apart from these, there are thousands of non-Microsoft newsgroups devoted to Windows tips and troubleshooting. It is impossible to browse them all for a specific topic so the best approach is to do a newsgroup search in Google: go to **www.google.com** and click the Groups tab. Type a description of your problem, bearing in mind that accurate keywords trigger the best results.

We tried *Windows XP reboots without warning* and Google returned 727 newsgroup postings. These would have been impossible to find in one lifetime merely by browsing.

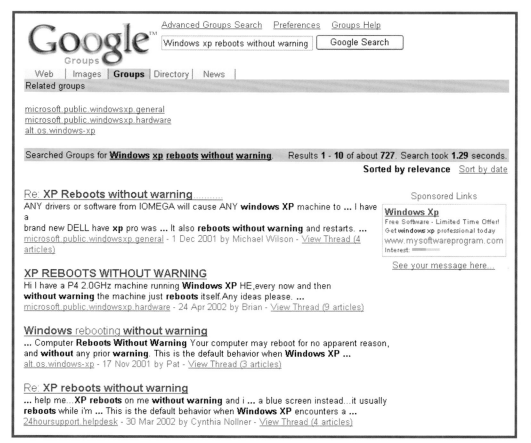

To search all newsgroups without leaving your web browser, use a Groups query in Google.

Real-time online assistance

If your searches aren't getting results, you can email a Microsoft support expert via the Microsoft website – but that support only applies to programs you bought separately from your computer. If your problem is with a program supplied with your PC – such as a copy of Windows that came pre-installed – you'll need to contact the PC manufacturer instead.

It's not a bad idea to visit the manufacturer's website anyway, as they often provide downloads for key bits of hardware –

usually because something was wrong with the previous device drivers. Every manufacturer's site is different but they all work in much the same way. For example, if you want to visit Dell support, head for **www.dell.com/uk** and then click on the Support & Help link. You can now browse the available support documents and downloads by system type, or click on the Windows XP or Windows Vista support centre icons for solutions to Windows problems.

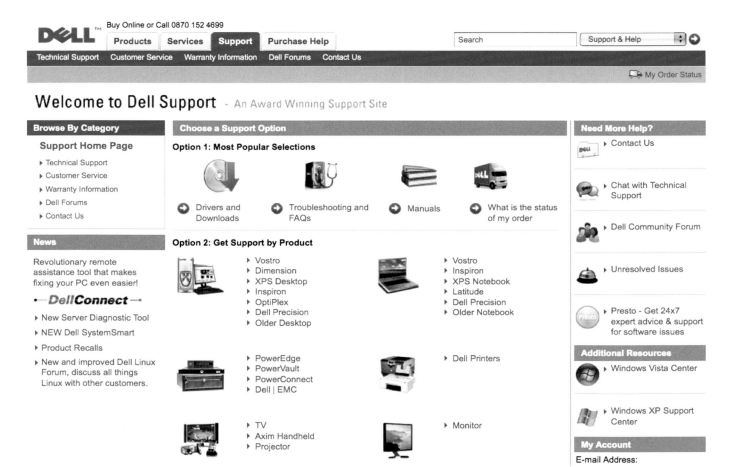

If Windows came pre-installed on your PC, you shouldn't email or call Microsoft for technical support – it's up to the PC manufacturer to take care of you.

General software troubleshooting techniques

Windows has not always enjoyed a reputation for stability and reliability and there is no disputing that Microsoft has in the past released software that was not fully de-bugged and which demanded too much of the humble machines of ordinary users. The arrival of Windows XP turned all this on its head because, despite initial teething troubles, it is a very stable operating system that is ideally matched to the powerful hardware found in even the most modest of today's home computers.

Users brought up on Windows 95 and, to a lesser extent, Windows 98 and Windows Me, grew to accept that they would be very lucky indeed if their computers went a whole week without crashing. Some users were resigned to rebooting several times a day and it was fashionable to lay the blame for every problem at Microsoft's door. In fact, snags were just as likely to arise because of poorly written third-party software, especially as software vendors were locked into competitive upgrade cycles in which they tried to release a major revision to every program every year without adequate time for testing.

Programs sometimes alert to the fact that an update is available. Others expect you to remember to visit the developer's website periodically.

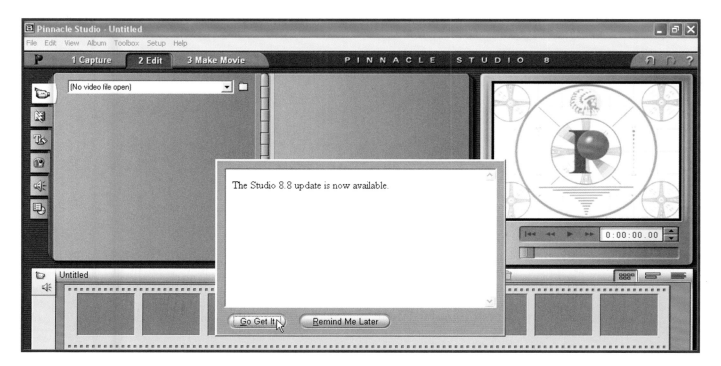

Now, as then, the cool way to play things is not to upgrade a program until:
a) the old version is no longer up to the job
and
b) the new version has been through the bug-blasting early stages and is generally regarded as reliable.

Assuming that your computer hardware is in good working order, day-to-day problems and error messages could be caused by Windows itself or by the programs you have installed within it. Here are some tips on identifying problem programs and whipping them into line.

● If a problem is signalled by a formal error message rather than a perfunctory shut-down or freeze, you will know which program issued the message because it puts its name, or at the very least its icon, in the title bar. You can learn how to handle the error by looking in the program's manual, using its Help menu, visiting the support section of the manufacturer's website, checking the postings in user forums or trying a general web search with your favourite search engine.

● If a program does not display an error message but is obviously not working properly (perhaps it won't print, play music, save files or display video), then the first thing to do is try performing the same actions in another program. This is a rudimentary but effective way of ruling out problems with Windows itself. If this leaves you still suspecting the program, you can search for a solution using any of the means described above. However, you may find it simpler to delete the offending program with the Add/Remove Programs feature in Control Panel and then reinstall it.

● Sometimes when you uninstall a program, not every trace is removed. References may remain within the Windows Registry and in the worst case it might prove completely impossible to delete a program because its entry has disappeared from the Add/Remove Programs list (even though its folders and files remain on the hard disk). A technique worth trying is to reinstall the program into the same folder and then try to delete it again. If this doesn't do

Q. When is an error not an error? A. When it is an idiosyncrasy, if this message from Excel is anything to go by. Other self-respecting Windows programs (including Word) have no problems with such a task.

Microsoft Excel

 A document with the name 'Accounts.xls' is already open. You cannot open two documents with the same name, even if the documents are in different folders.
To open the second document, either close the document that's currently open, or rename one of the documents.

 OK

the trick, you may need a third party uninstaller such as Norton CleanSweep (**www.symantec.com**) or a shareware alternative like Advanced Uninstaller Pro, from Innovative Solutions (**www.innovative-sol.com**).

● If the problem persists after reinstallation, it might be worth looking for a conflicting program on your computer's hard disk. A web search for the program's name together with the words 'conflict' and 'problem' usually delivers results. Two of the most popular CD burning programs, Easy CD and Nero 5, were notorious at not getting on together. (Easy CD had other problems too, but its replacement, Easy CD and DVD Creator, seems very well behaved.)

● If you use Windows XP or Windows Vista with software inherited from an earlier Windows system, you should check that the older software is compatible with your current version of Windows. One way of doing this is to make sure it has the Certified for Windows XP or Certified for Windows Vista logo, and another is to check out **www.xpsc.net** (for Windows XP) or **www.iexbeta.com/wiki/index.php/Windows_Vista_RTM_Software_Compatibility_List** (for Vista). Both sites are user-submitted directories of what works, and what doesn't. Microsoft has its own compatibility pages at **www.microsoft.com/windowsxp/home/upgrading/advisor.mspx** and **www.microsoft.com/windows/products/windowsvista/buyorupgrade/upgradeadvisor.mspx**. (Please note that 'Check for upgrade eligibility' redirects to the Vista upgrade advisor; 'Download the upgrade advisor' still downloads the correct software for XP.)

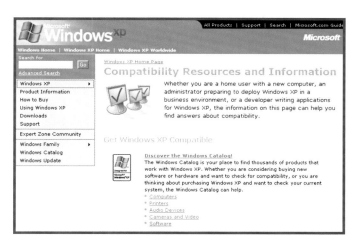

The trouble with Microsoft's XP compatibility catalogue is that it lists the programs that work and not the ones with problems.

● If you find that one of your programs isn't compatible with XP or Vista, all is not lost: the Program Compatibility Wizard may be able to help you

On Windows XP:

   Start

   All Programs

   Accessories

On Windows Vista:

   Start

   Control Panel

   Programs

   Use an older program with this version of Windows

The wizard will take you step by step through the process of making older programs work with your version of Windows.

In conclusion, never take a properly functioning computer for granted. Every time you add a new program, it has the potential to throw your existing software off kilter by replacing files on which the existing software depends. The golden rule is always to make a backup in Windows 98 or set a System Restore point in Windows Me and Windows XP before installing any new program.

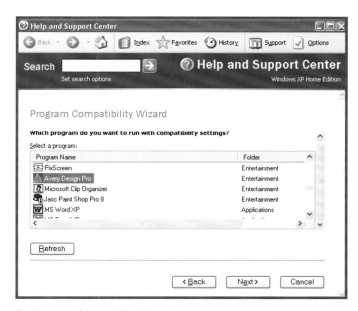

The Program Compatibility Wizard can't make an old program work any better than it used to, but it can stop it freezing and crashing.

PART

Windows Update

Microsoft does its best to make Windows perfect, but inevitably people find the odd bug or incompatibility long after the installation discs were manufactured. In order to fix the problems, Microsoft provides a range of updates via Windows Update. Some are critical, some are handy and others are pretty useless, but it's essential to keep an eye on the available updates to make sure you don't miss anything important.

Both Windows XP and Windows Vista can automatically check Windows Update for new downloads, but by default they're designed to do so in the wee small hours of the morning. Here's how to run Windows Update manually. In our screenshots, we'll be using Windows Vista but the process is the same on Windows XP.

You can launch Windows Update in two ways: by choosing Windows Update from Internet Explorer's Tools menu, or by clicking:

 Start

 All Programs

 Windows Update

Windows Update will automatically prioritise the most critical updates; if you click Install Now, it will install them and nothing else. However, it's never a bad idea to have a look at the list of updates. To do that, click on View Available Updates.

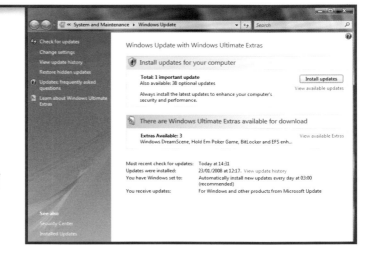

Windows Update doesn't just list fixes for Windows itself. It also tries to identify updated driver software for your hardware, so in this example we can see that there's a driver for our computer monitor. Other updates aren't necessary, such as the various language packs. In this case, all we need is the Windows Defender update, which Windows Update has already selected, and the new driver for our monitor – so we'll tick the box next to the Philips Electronics update and then click Install.

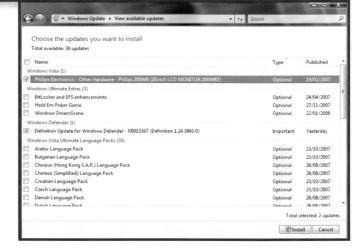

This screen gives us quite a lot of information. The most obvious bit is the progress bar that tells us what's happening – in this case, downloading an update – but immediately below that you can see when Windows Update will check for new downloads. In this case, it's the default setting, which looks for new updates at 3am. It's easy to change that: click on Change Settings in the left hand panel.

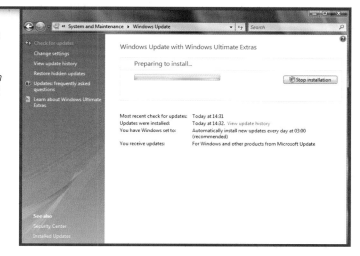

Unless your PC will actually be on at 3am, it's a good idea to change the installation schedule to a more sensible hour. We'd advise against changing the frequency to less often than daily, though, because if Microsoft discovers something serious such as a major security hole it issues an update immediately. The longer your PC goes without the update, the more vulnerable it remains.

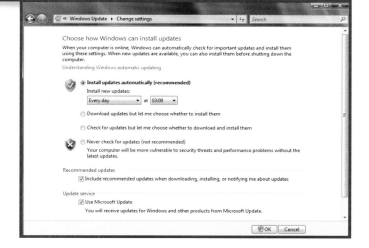

Help! Windows Update didn't work!

For most people Windows Update works fine, but occasionally you'll go through the process of identifying and downloading important updates only to discover that the installation failed. Why? Windows Update doesn't say. It just gives you an incomprehensible error message with an error number.

There are a number of reasons why this might happen – bugs in various bits of Windows, connection problems and so on – but in our experience the most common one is security software. For example, if we don't disable the BitDefender anti-virus software, every Windows Update we attempt ends in failure. If we disable it, try again and then re-enable the security protection, everything goes swimmingly. If that doesn't solve the issue, it's time to visit the Microsoft knowledge base to find the reason for the failure. Remember to take a note of the error code, as this will help to identify the problem.

PART

Internet, email and online tweaks

These days, a computer without an internet connection is like a car without wheels. The hardware we use to connect is pretty reliable but the same can't be said about software. Of all the PC problems we encounter, internet-related ones are the most common – and usually, the simplest to fix.

Connection problems

Most people connect to the internet in one of two ways: through a modem or through a broadband connection. There is a third method, wireless, which we'll come to later in this section. With modem connections, the software you need is usually provided on CD when you sign up with an internet Service Provider (ISP) and that software configures your computer to use the service.

With broadband, things are slightly different. You may have been given (or bought) a router, which is a bit more complicated than a modem – and troubleshooting router connections is slightly different to troubleshooting modem ones. In this section we'll look at both kinds of connection.

I can't get a connection!

If your modem is connecting to the internet but the site you want to visit isn't appearing, it might not be your internet connection: it could be that the site you're visiting is currently unavailable, in which case other sites should work fine. If you can't access someone's web page but Google works fine, the problem isn't at your end.

At other times, you'll find that you can connect but nothing

Messages displayed in the lower half of the Dial-Up Connections dialogue box provide reliable clues as to why a connection has failed.

Why you don't get the broadband speed you're paying for

We're sitting here with a super-speedy broadband connection, but we aren't getting anywhere near the speed we're paying for – and neither is anybody else. A typical 8Mbps broadband connection typically delivers half the advertised speed, and in many cases it struggles to deliver even that.

The reason for the disparity is that ISPs advertise the maximum possible speed of a connection, but real-world speeds are dependent on how far you are from the telephone exchange, how good the quality of your phone line is and how many other people in your street are using the same exchange. In practice, getting a full-speed connection is impossible, so don't be surprised if a site such as Think Broadband's speed tester (**www.thinkbroadband.com/speedtest.html**) tells you that your connection is much slower than you thought it was.

The difference between what the ads say and what you actually get has made a lot of people unhappy, and both the Advertising Standards Authority and telecoms watchdog OFCOM have been inundated with complaints. As this manual went to press, OFCOM was considering new rules that would compel ISPs to be more honest in advertisements.

The free *Speedtest.net* will check your broadband speed and let you know whether you're getting the speed you're paying for. In this screenshot, we're getting about 15Mbps, which is about right for a connection advertised as 20Mbps.

happens. Your email program says 'connecting' but doesn't do anything and your browser waits for a while before giving up completely. In that case the problem may well be at your ISP's end. It doesn't happen very often but it does happen occasionally and all you can do is wait for your ISP to fix whatever they've broken. If you absolutely, positively can't wait to get online, try using a different phone number and account in Dial-Up Networking to connect to a different ISP. For example, Free-dialup.net will connect you if you get your PC to dial 0845 123 2000 with the user name 'free' and the password 'dialup'.

If you can't get a connection at all, the culprit may well be closer to home. With modem connections, the Dial-Up Connection box that appears whenever you connect provides

valuable clues as to the problem. If the message says 'Dialing… Dialing… No dial tone', then your phone line is probably the problem. Pick up the phone and check for a dial tone: if you get one, it means the cable between your modem and the phone socket has probably been disconnected.

Another message tells you that Windows 'Failed to connect to remote computer. Could not detect modem'. In a few cases this means your modem is broken, but most of the time it means either the modem has become disconnected (or dislodged if it's a PC card modem in a laptop), unplugged or loose in its slot (in the case of PCI card internal modems). If the problem has only occurred since you installed another bit of hardware, such as another PCI card device, it may be a conflict between the two bits of kit. Use Device Manager to disable the new device and see if that makes the modem behave.

Another common error message is 'The computer you are dialing into cannot establish a dial-up networking connection. Check your password and try again.' This is rarely a genuine password problem, and usually means a failure of the authentication server – the computer that checks you have the correct user name and password – at your ISP.

Sometimes it is a password problem, and you can tell because the message is 'Verifying user name and password… unable to establish a connection.' Try retyping the user name and password and connecting again. Windows 95, Windows 98 and occasionally Windows XP sometimes 'forget' passwords even when you've ticked the Save Password check box.

A really annoying broadband problem

From time to time our broadband connection either slows to a crawl or simply stops working for no apparent reason. It turns out that the problem is with our broadband router and it's solved by unplugging its power cable, waiting for ten seconds and then plugging it back in again. It's a very annoying bug and a rare example where the oft-parodied technical support advice 'have you tried turning it off and back on again?' actually works.

If you are sure your modem is working, dialling the right number and using the correct user name and password, try rebooting your computer before dialling again. This might sort out any hardware conflicts and at the very least will ensure that no other program has claimed a communication port that your modem requires.

If you still cannot connect, then you must strongly suspect your ISP. The best way of confirming this is to try logging on to another service provider. Naturally you can only do this if you have previously set up such an account or if you have a CD-ROM to hand (perhaps from the cover of a magazine) which contains a setup program for a trial subscription. There is no shortage of service providers that run free basic internet access services, accessible for the price of a local telephone call and we strongly advise having one or more of these set up on your computer at all times, if only to test that your computer is working and to provide a fallback if your usual provider lets you down.

See also p108–110 for more on modem problems.

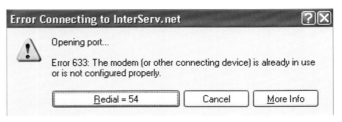

Error 633 is often caused by an earlier online session having failed to release system resources. In Windows XP, a reboot usually puts things right. However, in Windows 9x the message could indicate Registry damage (see Microsoft Knowledge Base article 191444).

Your connection is slow or unreliable

The number you were told to dial when you first established your account may no longer be the best one for you. Most ISPs have several numbers for each type of account (free access, unlimited access, or pay-as-you-go) and they add to these over time, especially if their user base continues to expand. If you experiment with different access numbers from the same ISP, you may find that dialling one number rather than another consistently provides a faster connection. Visit your ISP's website and check out the support FAQs. Make a note of all the available numbers for your category of service and then try them out.

One word of caution: if you have an 'any time' account (the sort where you pay a fixed charge each month and your calls are free), make sure you use only the designated dial-up numbers for this type of account – otherwise you will get a nasty surprise when your telephone company charges you for your internet calls.

Some ISPs offer an interactive facility to determine the best dial-up number for your computer. Others merely provide lists.

In Windows XP, to change the phone number that your modem dials:

 Start

 Control Panel

 Network and Internet Connections

 Set up or change your Internet connection

This opens the Internet Properties dialogue box. Open the Connections tab. Now, in the Dial-up and Virtual Private Network settings area, highlight the account you want to change and then click the Settings button. In this window, click the Properties button. You may now change the dial-up access number. If you also click the Alternates button, you can add backup telephone numbers and instruct your modem to try them one by one in the event that the primary number is engaged or dead.

In Windows 98, the procedure is almost identical but to get to the Internet Properties dialogue box you must use

 Start

 Settings

 Control Panel

 Internet Options

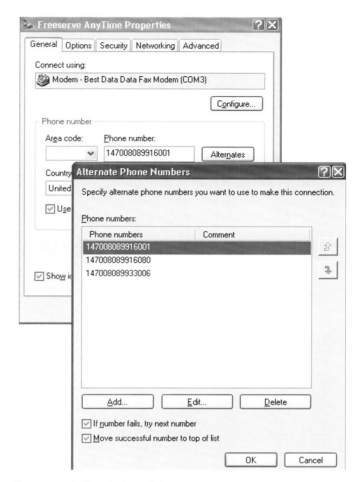

You can make it easier to switch between different dial-up numbers for your main ISP by adding alternative access numbers to the account instead of simply changing the existing number.

You successfully make a connection but lose it shortly afterwards

There are several reasons why this might happen. If you lose the connection after a fixed but relatively short period of time, typically 20 minutes, it is almost certain that Windows has been configured to disconnect you if your modem is idle for longer than a designated period.

To check this, follow the instructions in section 2 above (Your connection is slow or unreliable) but this time click the Advanced button when in the Settings tab. This opens Advanced Dial-Up settings, wherein you can set the time that must elapse before you are automatically disconnected. If you have an ISP subscription that offers unlimited access for a fixed fee, you will probably want to uncheck both disconnection options so that you are never disconnected through inactivity.

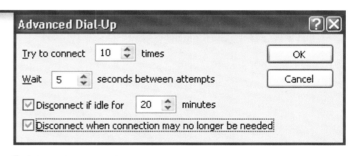

To ensure you are never disconnected inadvertently by Windows, remove the ticks from both disconnection boxes in Advanced Dial-Up properties.

If you are suffering disconnections that occur over a longer but still regular period, such as every two hours or three hours, it may be that your service provider automatically disconnects you after a fixed period of time. This is quite a common technique to prevent users hogging lines they do not need. It also encourages users to switch to broadband connections that generate more revenue for service providers. There is nothing you can do to prevent your connection being timed-out by the provider, apart from changing to an ISP who doesn't operate a cut-off policy, or redialling when it happens.

Other possible causes of dropped connections, apart from noisy phone lines, are unsuitable modem settings and the use of call waiting. To disable call waiting with most phone companies, you dial #43# (and *43# to reinstate it afterwards).

To check that your modem has not been set to disconnect after a period of idleness (this is a hardware setting made quite independently of the dial-up auto-disconnect feature described above), you should examine the modem in Control Panel and check its properties. To do this in Windows 98, use

 Start

 Settings

 Control Panel

 System

 Device Manager

Then click the plus sign next to Modem, select your modem and click the Properties button. Select the Connection tab and remove the tick from the *Disconnect* option.

In Windows XP, click Start and right-click My Computer. Now select

 Properties

 Hardware

 Device Manager

Click the plus sign next to Modem, right-click the name of the modem, and select Properties. Select the Advanced tab and then the Change Default Preferences button. If the *Disconnect a call* control is greyed out within Call Preferences, then your modem doesn't support hardware disconnection.

Of course, you may actually want to set a time limit for idleness, especially if you pay internet connection charges by the minute and are prone to leaving your computer online and racking up the bills.

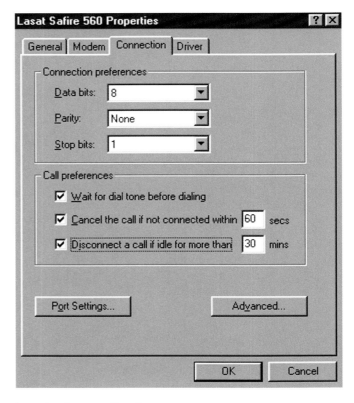

Accessing the properties of a modem in Windows 98.

The Windows XP approach to modem properties – not the easiest place to find.

Troubleshooting web page problems

You can encounter internet problems even when your connection is working fine. These are the most common errors you'll encounter – and what they actually mean. The latest version of Internet Explorer translates the error numbers into 'friendly' language, but older versions and other browsers may just display the error number.

Error 400 – The web page cannot be found
This error means that Internet Explorer can contact the website, but it can't find the actual web page. In most cases, this is due to a typing error so, for example, you might have typed 'mypage' when the actual file is called 'mypages'. Check your typing and try again.

Error 401 – Access Denied
The page you're trying to visit is password protected and you haven't provided the appropriate login details.

Error 403 – The website declined to show this web page
Internet Explorer can connect to the website, but something's preventing the site from showing the particular page. In many cases, you'll get this error because something's gone wrong with the website.

Error 404 – The web page cannot be found
The web page you've requested doesn't exist.

Error 405 – The website cannot display the page
This usually means the website owner has made a mistake in the way they've programmed a particular web page.

Error 408 – The operation timed out
This error is another sign of a site that's buckling under the weight of too many visitors. It means that the site is taking too long to respond.

Error 500 – The website cannot display the page
A 500 error is caused by one of three things: either there's a mistake in the way the website has been set up, the website is currently closed for maintenance, or it's exceptionally busy and has packed up under the load.

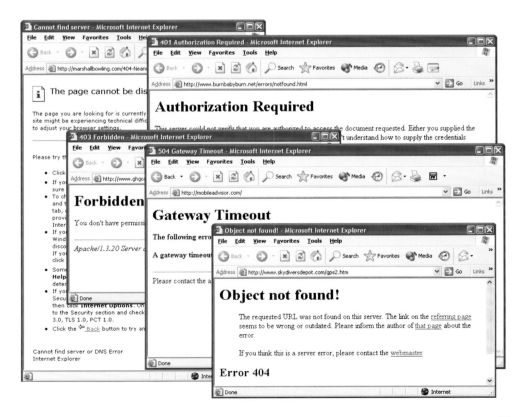

Surfing doesn't always go smoothly.

Troubleshooting internet video

The popularity of broadband has created an explosion in internet video, which can make even the dullest website more interesting. Unfortunately video isn't without its problems, and there are two key issues that come up again and again.

When I try to watch a video, the website says I don't have the right software

There are several different kinds of internet video and each one requires a different bit of software: to watch video in Windows Media format you'll need Windows Media Player, which comes with Windows; to see QuickTime movies, such as the movie trailers on the Apple website, you'll need QuickTime; to watch Flash videos, such as the ones on YouTube, you'll need to install the Flash Player; and to take advantage of services such as the BBC's 'listen again' service for radio, you'll need RealPlayer.

Even if you have these programs installed, you might still encounter problems: that's because video programs are updated frequently and websites tend to use the most recent version – so you might find that you have the right player, but not the right version.

You'll find the most up to date versions of the key video programs at these websites:

Flash Player	www.adobe.com/products/flashplayer
QuickTime	www.apple.com/quicktime
RealPlayer	www.realplayer.com
Windows Media	www.microsoft.com/windows/windowsmedia

Video clips are jerky and very bad quality

Video needs a fast broadband connection, so if you find the quality isn't up to much – assuming you're not accessing a really low-quality video clip – then connection issues are usually the cause. The website may be busy or you may be connecting at a peak time for your ISP; in both cases, it's worth trying a different website (where possible) or simply waiting until later on and trying again. If you have a wireless network, you may find that poor reception is the source of your worries. We'll discover how to fix that in the next section.

The BBC's iPlayer service is excellent, but you'll need to install the Flash Player to see streaming video and the RealPlayer if you want to use the Listen Again service for radio.

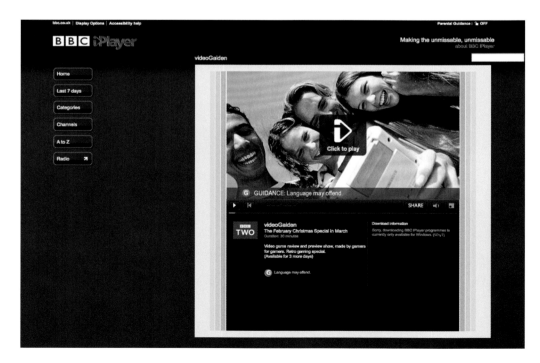

PART 2

Troubleshooting wireless networks

Wireless networks are wonderful – when they work. However, when they misbehave they can be one of the most frustrating kinds of computer problems to fix. The good news is that when you know what you're looking for, wireless problems don't take long to find and fix.

Wireless connection problems tend to fall into three categories: your wireless connection has mysteriously stopped working; your wireless connection has become very, very slow; or you can't get a wireless connection in the first place. Here's how to diagnose all three kinds of problem.

Before we start, though, the usual advice applies: make sure Windows itself is up to date via Windows Update and check with your hardware manufacturer to see if there's an updated device driver for your wireless equipment. In many cases, simply updating Windows and its drivers can make problems disappear forever.

When your wireless connection simply stops working

If you find that your wireless network stops working for no good reason, the first thing to do is to check whether you're still in range of the wireless router. To do this, look at the wireless icon in the system tray (at the bottom right-hand corner of the screen)

If your wireless signal isn't great or seems to be suffering from interference, use your router's browser-based control panel to change the wireless channel and see if that makes a difference.

Wireless Settings

Wireless Network

Name (SSID):   teh intarwebs!!!!

Region: Europe   ▼

Channel: 11 ▾

Mode: ▼

| 01 |
| 02 |
| 03 |
| 04 |
| 05 |
| 06 |
| 07 |
| 08 |
| 09 |
| 10 |
| 11 |
| 12 |
| 13 |

Wireless Access Point

☑ Enable Wireless Access Point

☑ Allow Broadcast of Name (SSID)

☐ Wireless Isolation

Wireless Station Access List   tup Access List

Security Options

○ Disable

◉ WEP (Wired Equivalent Privacy)

○ WPA-PSK (Wi-Fi Protected Access Pre-Shared Key)

○ WPA-802.1x

and hover the mouse over it. A little bubble should pop up showing whether you're getting a strong signal or not. If you aren't, try moving your computer to get a better signal. The more obstacles – walls, radiators and so on – between your computer and the wireless router, the worse the signal strength will be.

Interference can be a problem too. Some home devices, such as cordless phones, baby monitors, wireless video transmitters that send pictures from one room to another and even microwave ovens, generate radio waves on the same frequency as your wireless network. Make sure your router isn't close to a cordless phone base station or a microwave and consider changing channel on the wireless router. To do this, use the router's browser-based configuration screen and look for the Wireless Settings. You should now be able to change the channel. Disable and then restart your computer's wireless connection to see if things have improved.

If you're confident that the problem isn't the signal, you could try repairing the connection. In Windows XP, you'll need to have installed Service Pack 2 (which you should have anyway, because it contains lots of bug fixes and important security patches); in Windows Vista, the feature you need is already installed. Simply right-click on the wireless icon in the system tray and select Repair. This will reset your wireless connection and we've found it often fixes mysterious wireless problems – such as the wireless connection refusing to work when our system wakes from sleep mode.

Still no joy? If you have an external wireless adapter such as a USB or PC Card adapter, try unplugging it and plugging it back in again. This forces Windows to reset the wireless connection and, again, it often fixes mysterious wireless problems.

On Windows Vista, there's another thing to try. For no good reason, the Network Discovery feature – which enables your PC

We don't know why, but from time to time our copy of Windows Vista decides to turn Network Discovery off – which means it can't see any wired or wireless networks. You'll find this option in the Network and Sharing Center in Control Panel.

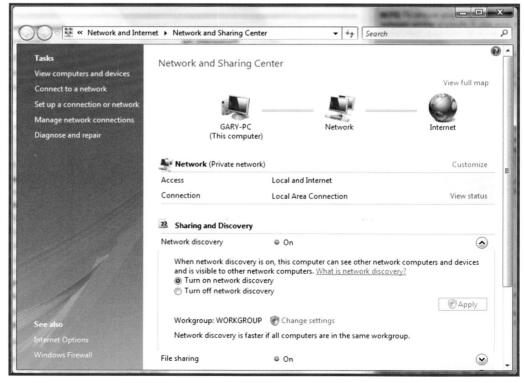

to find and connect to networks – sometimes switches itself off. To make sure that hasn't happened on your PC, go to Control Panel and then the Network and Sharing Center and make sure Network Discovery is switched on.

When your wireless connection slows down

If your wireless connection is getting slower and slower, check that it isn't just the website you're looking at – it sounds obvious, but we've often cursed our connection only to discover that the problem was with a website instead. If every single site crawls, your email takes forever and nothing seems to work very quickly, the culprit is usually your wireless signal. Wireless connection speeds drop dramatically with distance, so the closer you are to the wireless router, the faster your connection will be.

Another factor that affects wireless is other devices, so for example if you're using your PC while someone else connects to the same wireless router with their laptop, games console or mobile phone then the available connection speed is shared among everyone – so if there are three devices, you may only get one-third of the speed you might expect. This is particularly noticeable when you're connecting to public wireless networks, such as the ones in train stations, coffee shops and other public places: unless you're very lucky, the number of simultaneous users means connection speeds will be much slower than you might expect.

Other computers can affect your connection speed in a different way. These days, many wireless routers support several standards – so for example our router uses the 802.11g standard, but also supports the older 802.11b standard. That's generally a good thing, because it means you don't need to throw out older kit, but there's a potential problem there too: in many cases, if an 802.11b device connects to your wireless router, the router assumes every connection is 802.11b. Why does this

Many wireless routers support multiple standards, but older, slower kit can slow the entire network down. You can switch this support on and off in your router's control panel.

Wireless Settings

Wireless Network

Name (SSID):	teh intarwebs!!!!
Region:	Europe ▼
Channel:	11 ▼
Mode:	g & b ▼
	g & b
	g only
	Auto 108Mbps

Wireless Access Point

☑ Enable Wireless Access Point
☑ Allow Broadcast of Name (SSID)
☐ Wireless Isolation

Wireless Station Access List   [Setup Access List]

Security Options

◯ Disable
◉ WEP (Wired Equivalent Privacy)
◯ WPA-PSK (Wi-Fi Protected Access Pre-Shared Key)
◯ WPA-802.1x

matter? It's because different standards offer different speeds. 802.11b offers a maximum speed of around 11Mbps, but 802.11g is roughly five times faster – and in some cases, such as 'super G' routers, it's faster still. That means when your router drops down to an older standard, your speed suffers dramatically – and remember, that connection is shared between every device that's connected, so two computers connecting via 802.11b will share that 11Mbps connection. That means it's a good idea to switch off any wireless-enabled devices you don't need.

When you can't get a wireless connection at all

If you're at home, make sure you check the obvious things first. Is the wireless router switched on? Is your wireless adapter switched on too? It sounds silly, but many laptops have an external switch that enables and disables the wireless adapter, so if you have such a machine make sure the switch is in the correct position.

Device driver incompatibilities are a common cause of network problems, and it's easy to see whether that's the cause of your current difficulties. From the Start menu or desktop, right-click on My Computer and choose Manage. Under 'computer management' click on Device Manager, and then expand the Other Devices folder. If you see your wireless adapter in here, that means the drivers haven't been installed. The adapter should be in the Network Adapters folder: if it is, double-click on it, click on the General tab and look for a message telling you that the adapter is working properly. If it isn't, you'll see an error code here. Take a note of the code and search for it on the support section of the Microsoft website to find a fix for the problem.

If your wireless adapter doesn't appear in either Other Devices or Network Adapters it usually means one of two things: either the device drivers haven't been installed properly or there's a fault with the wireless adapter itself. With internal wireless adapters, make sure they're seated properly in the expansion slot (make sure the PC is unplugged when you do this!); with USB or PC card adapters, try removing and reinserting them.

Assuming both hardware and drivers are okay, it's time to look for other possible causes. If you can detect a wireless network but can't connect to it, try repairing the connection (as we

Make sure Internet Explorer isn't set to 'Always dial my default connection' if you want to access wireless networks. The option is under Tools > Internet Options > Connection.

described in the first part of this section). If that doesn't work, re-enter the password (if the network is password-protected). Windows has an annoying habit of forgetting network passwords occasionally, and you'll often find that re-entering your login details fixes the issue. If that doesn't work, reboot the wireless router by unplugging it from the mains, waiting 30 seconds and then plugging it back in again.

If you find you can connect to a public wireless hotspot but can't do anything – so for example your laptop says you're connected but your email doesn't seem to be working – the problem is usually financial rather than technical. Many public wireless services cost money, and you won't be able to do anything until you launch your web browser and either log in to your hotspot account (if you're an existing customer) or pay for your wireless access. The same thing applies in hotels: your computer can see the wireless network and connect to it, but you won't be able to do anything until you give the hotel permission to bankrupt you.

If you use a dial-up modem at home, you might find that Internet Explorer isn't interested in wireless networks when you're out and about. To solve this, launch your browser and then click

 Tools

 Internet Options

 Connections tab.

If the 'Always dial my default connection' is selected, change this to 'Dial whenever a network connection is not present'. This change means Internet Explorer will only try to dial your modem when it can't find a wired or wireless internet connection.

PART 2

Troubleshooting email problems

Email is pretty reliable these days, which makes it all the more annoying when it goes wrong. As with internet connections, the solutions are usually very simple: it's just a matter of knowing what to check. Here are the most common kinds of email issues – and their solutions. In this section, we'll use Windows Mail, which comes with every copy of Windows Vista, but other email programs work in the same way.

I can't get email at all

The first thing to check is your internet connection: can you access web pages? If you can't, the problem is with your connection rather than with your email.

If you're sure your connection is fine, go into your email program and look at the bottom right-hand corner. Does it say 'Working Online'? If not, Windows Mail is in offline mode – which means it won't check for mail at all. Simply double-click on where it says 'Working Offline' to put it into online mode or click File and uncheck Work Offline.

If that doesn't work, go into

 Tools

 Accounts

and check your account details are correct and that you've entered the correct server details, username and password. If that's all okay, the problem is almost certainly with your ISP. If your ISP or email provider has a webmail system that you can use via your web browser, see if you can use that. You'll often find that even when normal email is broken, webmail will continue to work.

My email freezes mid-download

'Receiving message 1 of 20', says your email program – and then nothing happens. More often than not that means somebody has sent you something massive. Even on broadband,

and fun, while helping to reduce risks and annoyances

Windows Mail has a 'work offline' option for when you don't have an internet connection. You can switch between online and offline mode by double-clicking this message at the bottom of the mail window.

🖥 Working Offline

big files can take a while to download. If you'd rather not wait, webmail can help: log in to your webmail service and see if you can spot the offending file. If it's something you don't want, you can delete it from within webmail.

My email program keeps asking me for my password

This usually means a temporary problem with your ISP's mail system. Double-check in Tools > Accounts that your login details are correct; if they are, you'll usually find that your ISP fixes the problem within a few hours.

My emails 'bounce'

It's very frustrating when you send an email and immediately receive an error message, but the causes are usually simple. Most of the time emails 'bounce' because the email address hasn't been entered properly, but there are other reasons too: some firms have very strict email filters that check for bad language and which occasionally bounce perfectly respectable messages, and some ISPs have a maximum message size – so if you try to send something that's too big, the ISP will simply bounce it back to you. Another common reason for bounced emails is that the recipient's email inbox is so full there's no room for anything else.

You can see exactly what's happened by reading the 'Undelivered Mail' message that's sent to you: scroll down and it will tell you exactly why your message wasn't sent.

Someone's sent me a big file but I haven't received it

This is the reverse of the bouncing problem – this time, an email somebody sends to you doesn't get through. Again, the answer will be in the undelivered mail report they receive – and if they didn't receive one, that means they haven't used the right email address.

If the file is too big for your ISP's email message limits, then the ISP will reject it. There's no way around this, but your friend or colleague can use a web-based, file-sending service, such as Dropsend (**www.dropsend.com**) to get the file to you. Instead of the file, Dropsend emails you a web link that you can click to download the file or files.

Messages don't display properly

Many websites and some email programs send email messages in HTML format, which is the same format that web pages are written in. That's good, because it means the messages can include nice designs and attractive images; however, it's also bad because HTML messages are a favourite of spammers, scammers and other degenerates. Many email programs, such as Windows Mail, block external HTML and images as a security measure. If you're sure you want to turn HTML and images back on, click

 Tools

 Options

 Security

and uncheck the 'Download Images…' option – although we'd strongly advise against it!

I can't open an email attachment

As with HTML email, email attachments are a security risk – in fact, most of the really nasty viruses of the last few years have spread by email. Because of this, many email programs block file attachments. Once again you can disable this option in

 Tools

 Options

 Security

but we'd advise against it: if someone wants to send you files, we'd recommend DropSend or similar online services.

If the file isn't blocked but simply won't open, that's usually because it's in a format your PC doesn't understand. For example, you can't open a PPT file if you don't have PowerPoint installed – although for most such programs you can download free file converters that enable you to open files even if you don't have the same software as the sender. In the case of PowerPoint, you can find the free PowerPoint Viewer program by searching **www.microsoft.com/downloads** for 'PowerPoint'.

Legitimate emails end up in my junk mail folder

Junk mail filters are an essential feature of any email program, but unfortunately they can and do get it wrong – which often means perfectly respectable emails are wrongly identified as junk mail and filed in the Junk folder. To avoid this happening in future, click on

 Tools

 Junk Mail Options

 Safe Senders

and enter the email addresses of friends, family or colleagues. This list overrides the junk filters and prevents those senders' messages from ending up in the junk folder. You'll find similar options in stand-alone junk mail filters, such as the junk mail protection in Norton or McAfee's internet security suites.

Some files are just too big to email, especially if the recipient's ISP has a limit on incoming message sizes. Use the free DropSend service to get around this: it stores your file and emails a download link instead of the entire file.

Windows Mail attempts to protect your PC by blocking potentially unsafe files and content, but sometimes this blocks legitimate things too. You can disable the features if you're sure incoming messages are safe.

Privacy and security

On the internet, security and privacy are two very different things. Privacy means keeping your personal information safe from snoopers, and security is all about keeping your system safe and sound. As we spend more and more time on the internet, both issues have become increasingly important.

Preserving your privacy

If you've ever shopped on a site such as Amazon.co.uk, when you come back you might find that it greets you by name and suggests a few things you might be interested in. It does this by placing a 'cookie' on your computer. This is a tiny text file that stores some basic information about you and enables the site to recognise you when you return.

Some cookies are very useful – Amazon's ones, the cookies that mean you don't need to re-enter your user name and password every time you check your Windows Live Mail, and the cookie that Google uses to check whether it should filter out smut from your search results. However, when you browse the internet you could end up with more cookies than you might expect. That's because many websites also run adverts and the advertising networks use cookies to track your movements – so

Use Tools > Internet Options > Privacy to specify whether your browser should accept cookies willy-nilly, or whether it should be more selective.

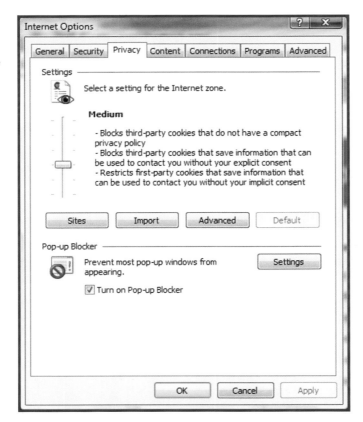

when you shop online you might not just get cookies from the website you're visiting, but from Adserver, Doubleclick and Fastclick.

It's easy to crack down on such cookies, though. In Internet Explorer, click

 Tools

 Internet Options

 Privacy

and you'll see a slider. This sets the security level and by default it's set to Medium. This setting blocks third-party cookies – that is, cookies from sites other than the one you're actually visiting – from sites that don't have a privacy policy and cookies that include information that can be used to contact you, such as your email address or phone number. If you click on Advanced, you can change the settings altogether, so for example you can block all third-party cookies irrespective of whether they have privacy policies or not.

Don't make your private data public

Many websites have a 'Remember Me' button that places a cookie on your computer and saves you having to log in every time you visit. That's very handy, but it's a very bad idea to tick such boxes if other people use your computer, or if you're using a shared computer such as one in an internet café. Even more importantly, if you're entering login details or passwords, say no when the web browser asks whether it should remember the password for future use.

In such cases, it's also a good idea to clear your browsing history when you've finished. This means someone else can't come along and visit the same pages you've just been looking at. To clear the browsing history go to

 Tools

 Internet Options

 General

and then click on the Delete button in the Browsing History section.

System security

The other thing to think about when you use the internet is system security. Recent web browsers do a much better job of blocking unwanted net nasties than before, but you can tweak the settings to suit your own requirements. Once again, it's time to go into Internet Explorer's Tools menu and select internet Options. This time, click on the Security tab.

Once again, you'll see a slider that shows your current security level and the default is Medium. This will warn you before downloading potentially unsafe content such as program files, and it will also block something called 'Unsigned ActiveX controls'. ActiveX controls are programs that run within the web browser; in recent years, malicious ActiveX controls have been used to spread viruses and other dangerous data.

If you're running Windows Vista, you'll see an additional option: Enable Protected Mode. If this isn't checked, check the box and restart Internet Explorer. Protected Mode is a Vista-only feature that keeps your web browser separate from your system, making it almost impossible for programs to infect your PC.

'Remember me' buttons on websites are handy, but don't use them if your PC is going to be used by other people or if you're using someone else's computer.

In Windows Vista, Internet Explorer has a feature called Protected Mode. Turn this off at your peril: it's a very solid way to protect your PC from internet nasties.

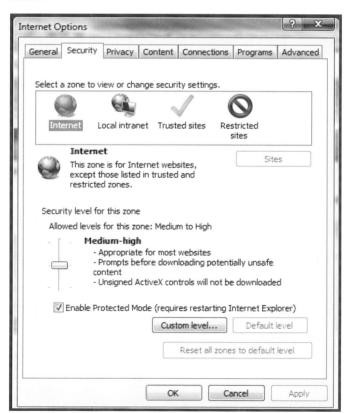

Dealing with internet infections

If your internet experience isn't ideal and you're sure the problem isn't with your connection, it's worth checking for infections – not just computer viruses, but all kinds of malicious software (malware). Malware is a real problem that causes countless headaches for computer users.

If your web browser is doing weird things, it's often because another program has changed it in some way. However, that doesn't necessarily mean your PC is infected. For example, if you install browser add-ons such as IE7Pro, which adds extra features to Internet Explorer 7, you'll find that the search bar no longer takes you to Windows Live Search. Instead, it takes you to a rebranded Google, which generates advertising income for IE7Pro's developers. It's perfectly legitimate and you can change the search settings in IE7Pro's options.

Other programs can get onto your PC by accident, because they came bundled with something else. The free – and wonderful – image viewer Irfanview (**www.irfanview.com**) installs the Google Toolbar unless you specifically tell it not to, which of course is fine if you want the toolbar but not so good if you don't. It's easy to address, though: in Internet Explorer just click on

 Tools

 Toolbars

and untick the Google Toolbar.

Other programs are less reputable, though. Many file-sharing programs – often used by people to get dodgy copies of music or movies – install all kinds of things, often without telling you, and the result is that adverts appear when you're trying to work, your home page is changed without your consent or your internet searches take you to a search engine you've never heard of. Getting rid of such programs is a pain, which is why it's always better to prevent them from getting on to your system in the first place. In this section, we'll find out how you can keep your system safe from online irritants – and we'll discover how you can find and fix problems if you suspect there's already something wicked in your copy of Windows.

Keeping net nasties off your system

You can avoid a lot of trouble by practising 'safe surfing'. That means you use the most recent version of your internet browser (at the time of writing, for us that's Internet Explorer 7) and keep Windows up to date, you never open email attachments you haven't asked someone to send you, you don't download software from sites of which you're not 100% sure, and you never install software you've found on file-sharing networks or disreputable websites.

Ignore any email that urges you to click on a link to update your system software and be very wary of any site that says 'you need to install X program to view our content'. With reputable sites, you don't need to worry – so, for example, you can happily say 'yes'

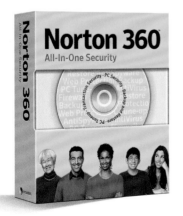

There are stacks of security programs available for PCs, ranging from free virus scanners to fully fledged security suites. If you have an internet connection, such software is essential.

when YouTube tells you that you need to install the Flash Player –
but if you have the slightest reason to doubt a site's trustworthiness
then don't install anything.

Unfortunately, safe surfing can't protect you against everything,
which means you'll need to invest in some security software.
Windows XP and Windows Vista both have some security software
built-in, but there are important omissions.

What you get in Windows – and what you don't

Both Windows XP and Windows Vista include a firewall, which is a
kind of electronic bouncer that's designed to prevent programs from
sneaking onto your PC without your express permission. In the case of
Vista, the firewall also blocks programs that are already on your PC
from using your internet connection, which is a handy way of
preventing some net nasties from doing their dirty deeds. However,
on Windows XP, the firewall only blocks incoming connections –
and on earlier versions of Windows there's no firewall at all. For such
systems it's a very good idea to invest in a dedicated firewall program,
such as the excellent – and free – ZoneAlarm. The free version is
tucked away in a quiet corner of the site, but you'll find it at
**www.zonealarm.com/store/content/company/products/znalm/
freeDownload.jsp**.

While firewalls are important, they only stop one kind of infection:
programs that sneak in through 'back doors' on your system. The
majority of programs try to get on to your computer in other ways,
usually by hiding themselves in downloads or email attachments. To
stop them in their tracks, you'll need anti-virus software and you
don't get that in Windows. There are stacks of companies offering
security programs – McAfee, Panda, BitDefender, Norton and so on
– but there are also free versions that do a decent job. We like AVG
Anti-Virus (**http://free.grisoft.com**) and AVAST (**www.avast.com**).

No matter which security software you go for, it's essential to keep
it up to date. All anti-virus programs enable you to download
updates so that they can find and fix the latest viruses. If you don't
use the updates, you could be lulling yourself into a false sense of
security: out-of-date virus software is better than no virus software at
all, but not by much.

So the firewall stops programs from sneaking in the back door
and anti-virus software ensures that you don't have any viruses.
Time to relax? Not yet. There's a third kind of malware, called
spyware, and it's often the most annoying of all.

What is spyware?

Spyware isn't the same as a virus, because most of the time you
install it deliberately – either by clicking yes on a website that asks
you to install a movie viewer or other goodie or by installing a program
that also includes spyware. Some spyware is relatively innocuous and
just displays adverts as you use the internet, but other spyware could
potentially be used by internet criminals to take control of your PC.
Even if it doesn't do anything nasty, it can still have a catastrophic
effect on your system: we recently checked the in-laws' PC to find out
why it had slowed to a crawl and we discovered 220 individual bits of
spyware on the system. Every single one of those programs was
running every time the PC was switched on.

In recent years, the amount of spyware targeting PCs has exploded
and it's estimated that an unprotected Windows XP PC will be
infected within 20 minutes of connecting it to the internet. If your
computer is doing weird things such as displaying unwanted ads
when you're not doing anything, disconnecting for no good reason or
generally slowing down, spyware may well be the culprit.

Keeping your system safe

On Windows XP and Windows Vista, everything you need to keep your system safe can be accessed from one place: the Windows Security Center, which you'll find in Control Panel. In this walkthrough, we'll use the Windows Vista version, although the Windows XP version is much the same.

The Security Center makes it obvious whether there are any security issues on your PC: if any of the lights are red, that means something needs your attention. To see more details of any category, click on the arrow to the right of the category name.

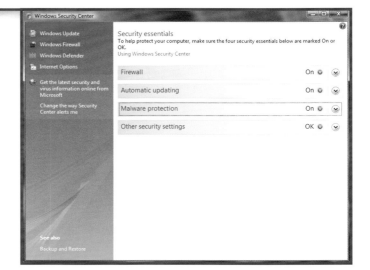

In this screenshot we've expanded all the categories and, as you can see, we've switched on the firewall, enabled automatic updates, installed anti-virus software – something that doesn't come with Windows – and enabled Windows Defender. You'll see links to the key programs (Windows Update, Windows Firewall, Windows Defender and Internet Options) at the top left of the window.

To see or change the firewall settings, *click on the Windows Firewall link and you'll see the window shown here. Click on the Change Settings button: the little shield next to the link is a reminder that you'll need to be logged in as the computer's administrator to make any changes.*

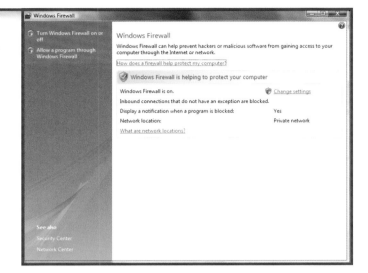

You'll now see the main Firewall status page. If you're connecting to an insecure network, such as a public one, it's a good idea to check the Block All Incoming Connections box. For home or office networks, though, it's fine to keep this option unchecked.

If you suspect that the firewall is blocking a legitimate program from connecting to the internet, click on the Exceptions tab to see which programs and services are allowed through the Windows Firewall. To add a program to the list, simply click on Add Program and then browse to the program file you want the firewall to ignore.

Nobbling net nasties

If you suspect you've contracted a net nasty, it's time to find it and fix it. We always look for viruses first and spyware second, because the former category can be much more destructive than the latter. If you've got anti-virus software on your computer, it's just a matter of launching it and clicking the Scan My System button; if you don't have anti-virus software, you can use an online virus checker for free. First, we'll look at a downloadable virus checker; then we'll show you how to use an online one.

Scanning for viruses

All anti-virus programs work in much the same way. In this walkthrough, we'll use the free AVG Anti-Virus from **http://free.grisoft.com** to scan our system for viruses and other malicious software.

Download and install the AVG software and then launch it from the desktop shortcut or from the Start menu. Before you can do anything you'll be asked if you want to check for updates. You do, so click on the Check... button.

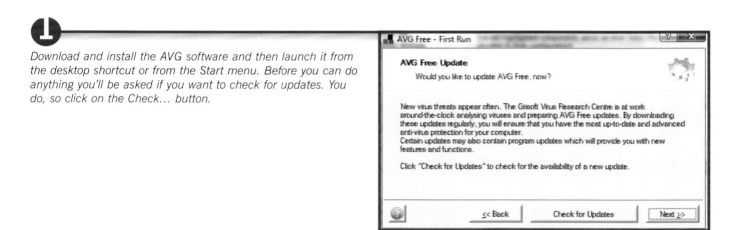

After a few seconds AVG will tell you what updates are available. Priority updates are essential, but if the dialog box only contains optional updates you can click Close quite happily. Here, though, there are a number of priority updates, so we'll click the Update button.

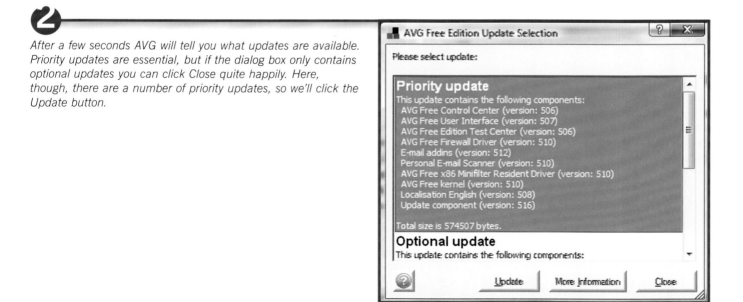

The dialog box will now show the progress as each update is downloaded and installed. Don't close this window until AVG tells you it's safe to do so!

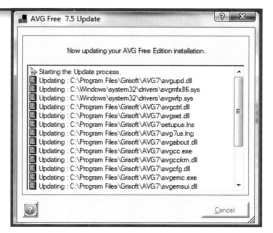

If you like, AVG can scan your system every day. There are two options: low priority, which runs in the background and lets you get on with things, and High Priority, which takes less time but tends to slow down your PC. We'd recommend the Low Priority option.

Click on Next and AVG will ask if you want to scan your system right now. That's always a good idea when you've just installed security software, so click on the Scan Computer button.

The next stage takes a while, because AVG needs to scan your entire system. If it spots a virus, it will pop up a warning and ask whether it should disinfect or delete the file, but if everything's hunky-dory you'll see the cheerful 'no threats found' message shown here.

Using an online virus scanner

You don't necessarily need to download anti-virus software –
although we'd strongly recommend it. Security firms such as
McAfee (**www.mcafee.com/freescan**) offer free online virus
scanners that you can use if you're in a hurry or if you suspect
that your virus software isn't spotting something it should.

*When you try to access McAfee Freescan using Internet Explorer
7, the page won't load. Instead, you'll get this message. That's
because Internet Explorer is a little bit paranoid and won't install
anything without your permission. Click on Close.*

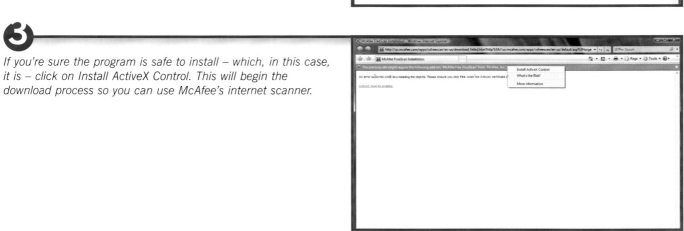

*At the very top of the web page window you'll see the
Information Bar, a yellow strip that runs the width of the browser
window. If you want to install the program Internet Explorer has
just blocked, click where it says Click Here To Install.*

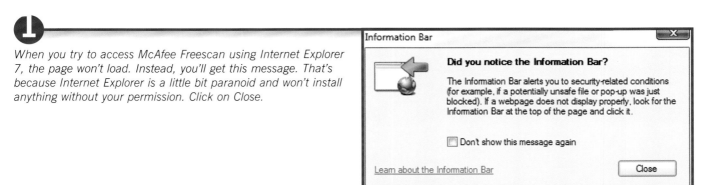

*If you're sure the program is safe to install – which, in this case,
it is – click on Install ActiveX Control. This will begin the
download process so you can use McAfee's internet scanner.*

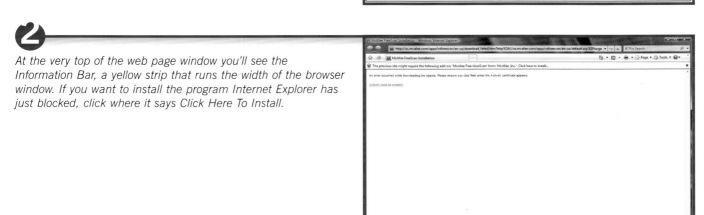

You will now be asked yet again whether you're sure about this and, to help you decide, Internet Explorer tells you what the program is and who made it. Click on Install to continue.

If you have other security software installed on your PC you may now get a message like this one, which comes from our copy of Spybot S&D. Clicking on Deny Change will prevent the McAfee scanner from operating, so we'll select Allow Change.

And here's the result: a virus scanner running inside our web browser. In the left-hand panel, you can specify which bits of your system to scan. We'd recommend scanning your entire hard disk, so select Drive C and then click on Scan.

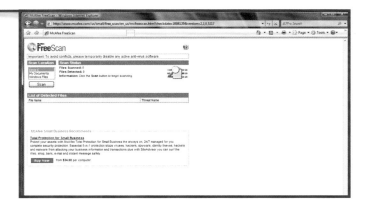

This would be a good time for a cup of tea, as even scanning the fastest computer takes ages. The scanner will show you its progress and, like any other anti-virus program, it will make it abundantly clear if it finds a nasty. If it does, you can then choose to disinfect the infected file or files.

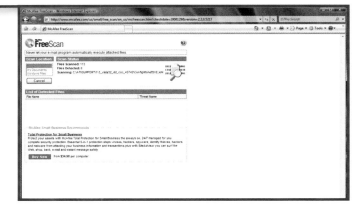

Now for the spyware. Windows Vista comes with a program called Windows Defender and it's also available as a free download for Windows XP. With Defender, scanning for spyware is simple.

Scanning for spyware with Windows Defender

Windows Defender comes with every copy of Windows Vista, and you can download a version for Windows XP from Microsoft.com/downloads. Once you've installed it, launch the program by clicking on the Start menu, navigating to All Programs and then clicking on Windows Defender.

Windows Defender isn't available for my system!

If you don't have Windows Vista or Windows XP, don't despair: programs such as the excellent and free Ad-Aware (**www.lavasoftusa.com**) run on Windows 2000, while Spybot – Search & Destroy (**www.safer-networking.org**) supports Windows 95, 98 and Windows Me. In this walkthrough, we'll run Spybot – Search & Destroy on our Windows Vista system, but the process is the same on any PC.

It doesn't look very exciting, but the main Defender screen provides some useful information: when you last scanned for spyware (if applicable), when Defender plans to do its daily automated scan, whether real-time protection (which can spot spyware the second it appears) is on, and when its list of nasties was last updated. You can change these settings by clicking on Tools, but for now we'll click on Scan.

Once again it's time for a cup of tea, as a full system scan can take anything from a few minutes to more than an hour if you've got a packed hard disk. If Defender spots anything, it will give you the option to remove the spyware. It's important to note that some programs, such as file-sharing software, may stop working if you disable their annoying advertising systems.

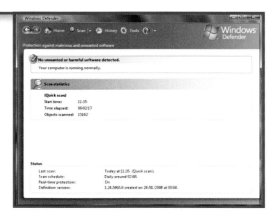

Ideally, at the end of a scan, you'll see this message, which tells you that Windows Defender has scanned your system and didn't find anything dodgy. If spyware was spotted during the scan it will detail that here, together with details of what – if anything – you told it to do with the spyware.

Scanning for spyware with Spybot – Search & Destroy

Spybot – Search & Destroy (Spybot-S&D) is available for Windows 95 onwards, and you can download it for free from **www.safer-networking.org**. Unlike many programs there are a few things you need to decide as it's installing.

During installation Spybot will provide you with a number of choices. If you're running Windows Vista, it asks whether it should enable Security Center integration, so Spybot appears in the Windows Security Center. This is generally a good idea. No matter what version of Windows you have, make sure Download Updates Immediately is ticked.

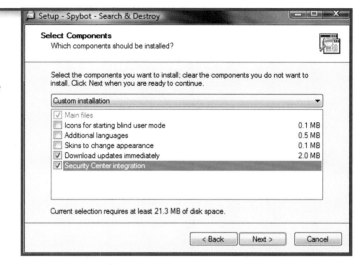

More choices, this time about what additional modules Spybot should install. SDHelper keeps an eye on Internet Explorer for any attempted infiltration by spyware and TeaTimer does the same for Windows. We'd recommend installing both.

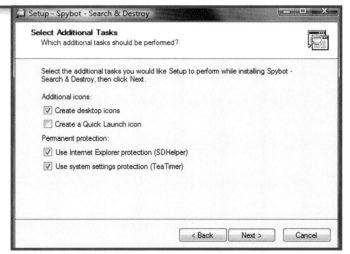

Once installation is finished you can choose whether or not to launch Spybot itself and whether the additional components should be enabled. If you choose yes to all the options you'll get a couple of information windows before Spybot itself appears.

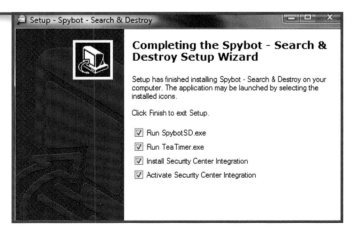

Before you can do anything, the Spybot-S&D Wizard appears. Whatever you do, don't be tempted to skip the Search for Updates step: new spyware is released all the time, so it's essential to ensure that Spybot knows about the latest threats.

You'll be asked to choose a download location for the update files. If you've got a broadband connection it really doesn't matter, but on modem connections the nearer the download location the faster it's likely to be.

We're nearly ready to scan, but first Spybot wants to know if it should install its system protection features, which it calls Immunization. Click on Immunize This System to continue.

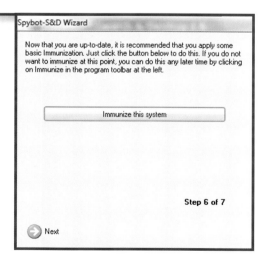

Now that all the optional bits have been configured you'll see the main Spybot window. To scan your system, click on the Check for Problems button.

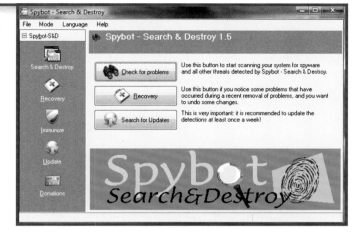

Guess what – it's time for tea again. Spybot will now scan your system for any spyware; if it spots anything, it will tell you what it is, where it lives on your computer and who made it. You can then choose to remove the offending software or, if it's something you know about and want on your computer, leave it alone.

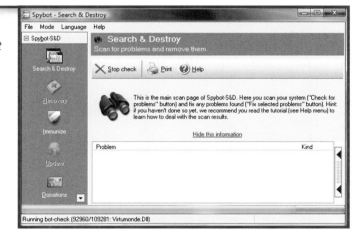

When the scan is over, Spybot will provide a summary of what it found. In this case we can do a happy dance because our system is spyware-free.

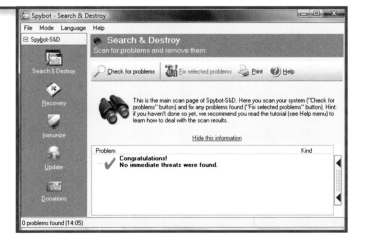

3

PART 3

Hot hardware hits

In this section, we focus on common hardware problems. This is necessarily a rather hit and miss affair, but if we attempted to cover all conceivable bases we would still be writing it – and you would be unable to lift (or afford) the resultant manual. If your computer develops a more exotic flaw that we fail to explore, or even mention, apologies in advance. However, the strip-and-rebuild approach in Parts 4 and 5 will help you get to the bottom of virtually any computer conundrum.

Audio problems

Your computer's audio output, if any, is produced either by a microchip embedded on the motherboard or by a plug-in expansion card called, unsurprisingly, a sound card. Audio signals are then relayed to a set of speakers or headphones, enabling your computer to play standard audio CDs, music files (like MP3 and WMA files), DVD movie soundtracks and any variety of bells and whistles found on web pages. Windows also provides a selection of sound themes that make using your computer a more friendly and, arguably, intuitive experience, beginning with a tune when you first switch on, ending with another when you switch off and with all manner of sound effects in between. When this cacophony becomes suddenly mute, you know you have sound card or speaker problems.

Multi-channel surround sound speaker systems complement powerful sound cards but add complexity to connections.

Troubleshooting techniques

● When checking audio output, make sure that your computer at least looks as if it is producing sounds, even if you can't hear anything. For instance, pop an audio CD in the CD-ROM drive and set your music playback software in action. You wouldn't be the first to emerge from under the table having tried 20 different cable combinations only to discover that the PC was sitting silently without a sound to play.

All may be mute but you can only test your sound card and speakers when the computer is actively producing audio.

● Now check the cable connections. This may be no easy task with a surround sound system where satellite speakers connect to a subwoofer rather than directly to the computer, so dig out the manual and double-check both the correct layout and your connections. It is essential that each speaker is connected to the correct channel on the subwoofer and that the subwoofer is correctly connected to the sound card. Colour coding may or may not help. Give each cable a shoogle (the technical term for an exploratory shake) while the computer is ostensibly, but mutely, playing music.

Most speakers these days, even simple stereo affairs, are self-amplified and require a separate power source. Check the obvious factors: are the speakers plugged in, are they turned on, do the lights come on, has the fuse blown, etc.?

Hooking up speakers to a sound card can be complicated when a subwoofer is involved. Take the time to check that each channel is correctly connected.

- Check the volume controls on the subwoofer – there may be several – and, if your sound system was shipped with a further volume control on a cable, ensure that it is plugged in and turned up.

Volume controls at the hardware end, as opposed to software settings on your computer, can easily be muted by mistake (or by meddlesome under-desk toddlers).

- Test different types of audio output. One very common problem is having the volume control in a software music player turned right down or set to mute. Check the controls and if you have more than one multimedia player installed – Windows Media Player (supplied with Windows) and Winamp **(www.winamp.com)**, say – try both.

Software volume sliders are easily missed or set to zero.

- A related 'fault': if sound comes out of one speaker but not the other, check your software player settings. Ten-to-one says that the stereo balance control has been shifted to one side or the other.

Keep an eye on balance controls. Here the slider has been shifted all the way to the left, leading to lopsided output.

- Try playing non-musical files on your computer to eliminate software player problems. In Windows 98:

 Start

 Settings

 Control Panel

 Sounds

In Windows Me:

 Start

 Settings

 Control Panel

 Sounds and Multimedia

In Windows XP:

 Start

 Control Panel

 Sounds, Speech, and Audio Devices

 Sounds and Audio Devices

In Windows Vista:

 Start

 Control Panel

 Hardware and Sound

 Sound

 Change System Sounds

Now test some elements of the Windows sound scheme. If you can hear them, there is nothing much physically wrong with your sound card or speakers, and the problem almost certainly lies with software settings: either your multimedia player program or the sound card's drivers have likely gone awry. Try reinstalling both.

- While still in this area, look at the system volume control. This is located on the Sound tab in Windows Me and on a separate Volume tab in Windows XP. In Windows 98, you need to open the Multimedia folder from the Control Panel and look in the Audio tab.

Check the box that places a volume icon in the Taskbar – this is handy regardless of troubleshooting – and ensure that the volume has not been set too low.

Here you can send a volume control shortcut to the Taskbar (if it is not there already).

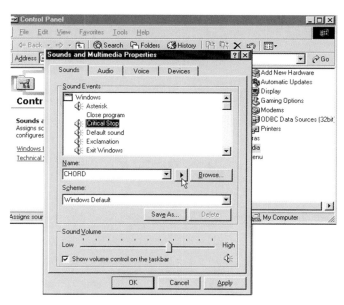

Windows provides plenty of sounds to play with. These are ideal for diagnostic testing.

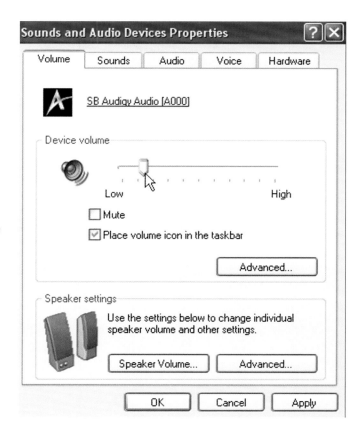

- If you now click the volume control icon in the *Taskbar*, up pops a slider that controls the overall system volume.

Double-click the icon for a full set of sliders that together control all varieties of audio output. This is your sound card's mixer utility. The precise settings here depend on your hardware configuration and your particular brand of sound card, but experiment with all the options and make sure that no relevant sliders are set to zero.

- You can tell your computer what kind of speaker set up you have to help it configure the best playback settings. In Windows Me:

 Start

 Control Panel

 Sounds and Multimedia

 Audio tab

 Sound Playback section

 Advanced button

In Windows 98:

 Start

 Control Panel

 Multimedia

 Audio tab

 Sound section

 Advanced Properties button

In Windows Vista:

 Start

 Control Panel

 Hardware and Sound

 Sound

Manage Audio Devices

Windows XP users can click the Change the speaker settings button from the Sounds, Speech, and Audio Devices window in the Control Panel.

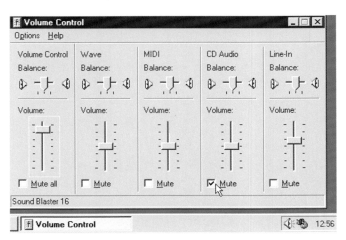

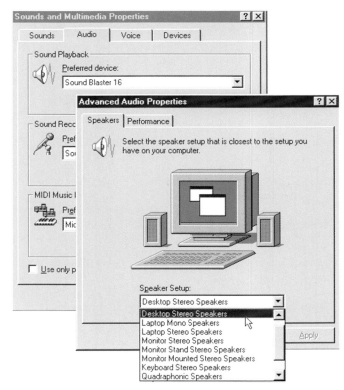

● Try connecting headphones to your sound card's speaker sockets. If you now hear sound, you know that the problem is with the speakers, not the card. Note that you may need to purchase an adapter to connect standard hi-fi headphones to the small 3.5mm audio socket on a sound card.

A cable/jack adapter lets you connect hi-fi headphones to a sound card.

● Substitution testing is a sure-fire way to pinpoint problems. If possible, transfer your speakers to another computer and see if they work normally. This would indicate a sound card or software problem back on the original computer. Also try connecting a different set of speakers to your computer.

● An old favourite: have you by any chance connected your speakers to your modem rather than the sound card? If we had a penny…

● If your computer has two sets of audio sockets, as is the case in a system equipped with both an integrated motherboard sound chip and a separate sound card, bear in mind that only one set will work at any one time. In virtually every case, the sound card, if present, will be active and the integrated chip passive. If your speakers are connected to the sockets provided by the motherboard, they will remain mute – so connect them to the sound card instead.

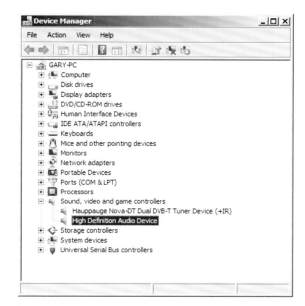

Some computers have integrated audio on the motherboard, like the one shown here. If you also have a sound card installed, Windows should use it and the sockets for the integrated audio will be disabled.

● If you are fortunate enough to have the option of swapping to an integrated chip, this is an easy way to diagnose or rule out sound card problems. The settings that control whether a chip or a card handles audio output are actually buried within the BIOS Setup program, so see Appendix 1 for details.

Enable the integrated audio option, connect your speakers to the appropriate sockets and run through the obvious tests described above. If you now hear sound, we would suggest swapping back to sound card output in BIOS, reconnecting the speakers to the sound card, and trying again. Still no sound? The sound card itself is almost certainly to blame.

● The trouble with sound cards is that they typically require several different drivers, any one of which may 'break'. You can see the full array in Device Manager (see p27 for directions).

Sound cards are relatively complex affairs with multiple functions and a driver set to match.

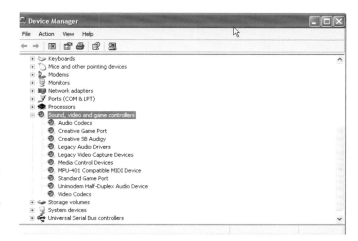

● If you suspect a driver problem or if Device Manager indicates one with an exclamation point or cross, you have two choices: reinstall the software over the top of the current drivers, or remove the existing drivers and start afresh. In our experience, the latter course is generally more profitable.

You don't have to physically remove the sound card at this point: simply uninstall it virtually with Device Manager.

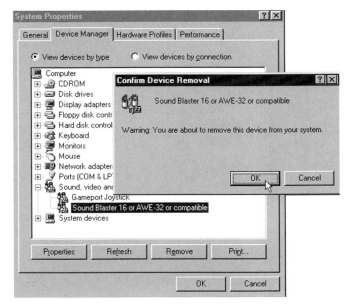

You can un- and reinstall a sound card in Device Manager without the use of a screwdriver.

● In Windows 9x, locate your sound card in the Sound, video and games controllers section of Device Manager and click the Remove button. In Windows XP, right-click your sound card's entry in the Device Manager list and select Uninstall. When Windows restarts, it will reinstall the sound card drivers afresh. Have your installation CD to hand. Better still, visit the sound card manufacturer's website and download updated drivers.

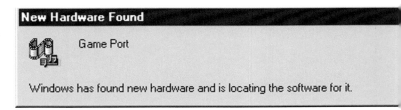

After uninstalling sound card drivers in Device Manager, Windows detects the 'new' hardware automatically next time you restart your computer.

● If you have problems with an ISA-slotted sound card (see p128), Windows won't automatically detect the 'new' hardware when you un- and reinstall drivers in Device Manager. You should therefore reinstall drivers from scratch using your original installation CD-ROM or, preferably, updated drivers.
A better bet – a much, much better bet, in our opinion – is dispensing with the card's services altogether and treating yourself to a PCI sound card instead. Windows handles PCI resources much more elegantly than ISA resources and conflicts are comparatively rare.

● Check the (All) Programs menu for applications, guides and troubleshooters that were installed along with the sound card hardware. You may just find the help you need there. In particular, you may find a diagnostic program that tests the sound card's playback and broadcasts a series of test signals to the speakers. If no faults are found with the card, this would tend to point to a speaker – or more likely a cable connection – problem.

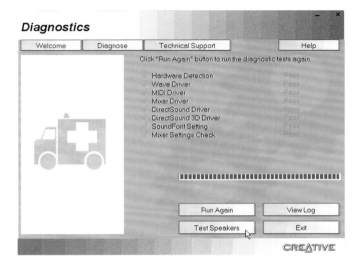

Sound cards often come with diagnostic utility software.

● When audio problems are apparent when playing games but not otherwise, run the Windows DirectX utility

 Start

 Run

 dxdiag

Open the Sound tab to diagnose and text DirectX features.

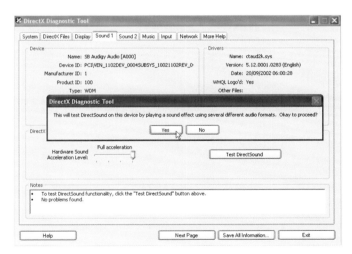

The DirectX diagnostic utility helps root out problems with game soundtracks.

● If all else fails, uninstall the sound card drivers in Device Manager and then physically remove, clean and replace the card in its slot (see p132 and p144–146 for help with this). Check that any internal audio cables are in place. For instance, CD or DVD drives may be connected to the sound card with skinny cables and delicate plugs and one may have shaken loose. This would account for a loss of audio CD playback, but would not affect other Windows-produced sounds.

   If you still have no luck, try installing the card in a different slot, even if it means temporarily removing another card to free up space. If – and only if – you have established that your speakers are okay, this would confirm a terminal sound card fault.

Video problems

Either you see an image on your monitor screen when your computer is switched on, or you don't – and if you don't, the problem lies either with the monitor or the video card/integrated chip. Simple as that?

In a word, yes. We cover the procedure for testing monitors on p105–107, but it really boils down to hooking it up to another computer to determine for sure whether it is alive or dead. Monitors do die, unfortunately, and CRT models also gradually lose brightness and contrast over time. In a corner of this room, for example, we have a 19-inch monitor that gave up the ghost suddenly precisely one week after the expiry date on its three-year warranty – conspiracy theory, anybody? – and a 15-inch model dating from 1995 that still works, but only just, i.e. its display is dull and indistinct to the point of uselessness. Monitor repair is generally impossible or too costly to be worthwhile.

When it comes to video cards, or video chips integrated on the motherboard, problems can be harder to pinpoint. However, in our experience they can almost always be remedied with a driver update, patch or reinstallation.

Never neglect the obvious. This monitor's brightness and contrast are controlled by a wheel located out of sight under the screen which can be all too easily snagged on the keyboard and adjusted by accident.

Troubleshooting techniques

- The key area for video issues is Display Properties and the easiest way to access it is by right-clicking the Desktop and selecting Properties from the context menu.

  For starters, you can reduce the colour depth and/or screen resolution with the Settings tab. There is often a compromise to be struck here, as many video cards can either display a fantastically high resolution or a fantastically high number of colours, but not both simultaneously. Older cards in particular will struggle if you run them too hard. If windows take an extra moment to pop up on screen and video playback is jerky, try lowering one or other setting to ease the load.

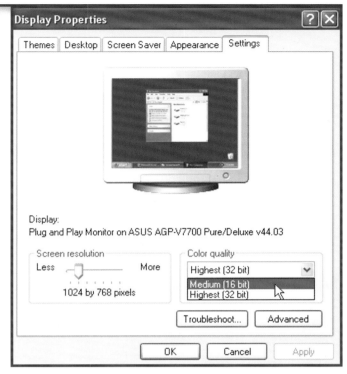

Reduce either the colour depth ('quality') or screen resolution, or both, to give an under-powered video card a break and make performance smoother.

- Still in the Settings tab, click the Advanced button and look in the Adapter and Monitor tabs. Here you should find the correct video card/chip and monitor listed i.e. the details should match your hardware. If not, install the correct drivers. In Windows 9x, click the Change button and follow the instructions. In Windows XP, click the Properties button and then use the Driver tab. Have any driver software that came with your monitor to hand, or visit the manufacturer's website and look for an update. If you have recently downloaded an updated driver file, point the wizard to this location now; otherwise, pop the original floppy disk or CD-ROM in the drive when prompted. Some driver updates are supplied as self-installing files that do all the hard work for you.

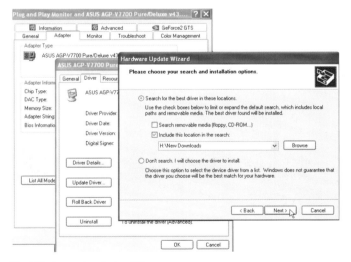

The Windows wizard simplifies driver installation; just tell it where to look.

- You may also find some useful additional information when you click the Advanced button in Display Properties. This can be very helpful when trying to establish whether or not you have the most up-to-date drivers.

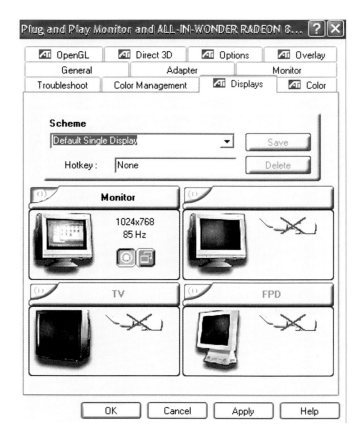

The look and layout of Display Properties (click the Advanced button) is determined by the video card drivers. Roam from tab to tab and experiment with different options to troubleshoot or improve display problems.

- As a rule, new drivers are made available only when there is some tangible benefit to be had from an upgrade, such as improving gameplay or fixing bugs. So if, for instance, you find that your monitor occasionally goes blank for a second or two, a driver update may be all that is required.

This information tab tells us the driver filename (version 43.45A). It also provides a link directly to the video card manufacturer's download web page. Click this and...

...we learn that an updated driver (version 44.03) is indeed available for download. Always be careful to grab the right driver for your hardware and operating system.

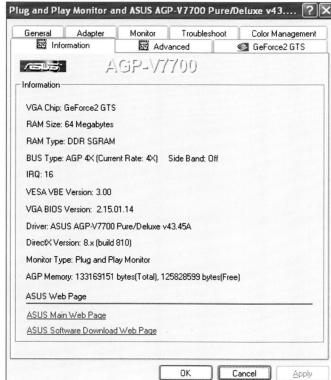

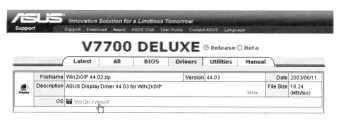

- If Display Properties leaves you in the dark, check the software that shipped with your video card, if you installed it yourself, or otherwise dig out the box of disks that came with your computer. You may well find a software utility or two that can help with information and diagnosis.

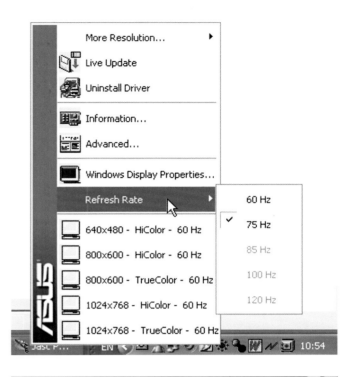

This particular video card came with a handy utility that sits in the Taskbar and provides information on demand.

- If you detect a slight but irritating flickering on your screen or if you get a headache or eye strain after a prolonged period in front of the monitor, check the refresh rate. This determines how frequently the video card redraws the images you see on screen and should be set to the highest value that the monitor supports.

  Do check the monitor manual first and don't set the refresh rate too high: while a video card may happily refresh the image 100 times per second (100Hz), this would potentially damage a monitor that supports a maximum rate of 75Hz. As a rough guide, a 60Hz refresh rate is too low for comfort, 75Hz should produce a stable image, and 85Hz or higher is rock steady.

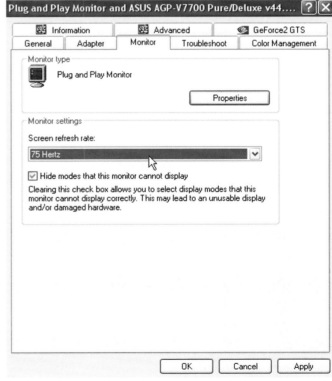

Set the refresh rate as high as your monitor will allow for a steady on-screen image.

- If you have just installed an old AGP video card in a newish computer, or a new AGP card in an oldish computer, and can't get it to work, this may be down to differing voltage requirements between the card and the slot. For instance, older AGP 2x-speed slots were designed for video cards that operated on a 3.3V supply, whereas faster 4x-speed and 8x-speed slots are designed for 1.5V cards.

- Although AGP video cards offer by far the best graphics performance and are essential for games-playing, most people can actually get by quite happily with a PCI-based video card. So, if your AGP card goes on the blink, or if the video chip embedded on the motherboard calls it a day (unlikely), don't necessarily assume that you must replace like with like. PCI cards are decidedly out of favour these days but you should find a small but adequate – and, compared to AGP, cheap – selection in any computer retailer.

  As we mention on p137, a spare PCI card is also a valuable troubleshooting tool. You may need to change BIOS settings if switching from AGP to PCI (see Appendix 1).

- Don't panic if your CRT monitor starts displaying strange patches of colour or psychedelic patterns. Almost certainly, its display is being affected by a strong magnetic source, so work out what this is (even speakers can affect a screen), move it away and 'degauss' the screen. See the monitor manual or on-screen menu for instructions on how to proceed.

A PCI-based video card is fine for most needs. A card with 16MB of onboard memory is sufficient; 32MB is better.

- If when you restart your computer the monitor remains completely blank, try disconnecting the keyboard and rebooting. Sometimes a keyboard fault can halt a system right at the outset.

  The next test is to connect a different monitor that you know to be good. Of course, you might not have a spare working monitor to hand, nor the means to borrow one. However, you might still be able to hook up your computer to a television set if the video card has S-Video or composite outputs and the TV has compatible inputs. This would at least confirm that the video card is working.

An S-Video input/output socket like this may enable you to connect your computer to a television set.

- To establish for sure that your monitor is dead, test it with another computer. If that isn't possible, we would suggest having a word with a friendly local computer parts retailer. Explain the problem and ask whether they would be prepared to test your monitor if you brought it in – a test that should take all of 30 seconds. By all means make it clear that you will give the shop the business if it turns out that you need a new one.

  Pay attention to the monitor data cable, too. Bent pins in the VGA connector, perhaps caused by the weight of a heavy monitor cable gradually pulling the plug out of its socket, can kill a display. Very fine, pointy-nosed pliers should suffice to bend them back into place.

  Unfortunately, the other end of the data cable is likely to be moulded to the monitor chassis and completely irremovable. If you suspect that your cable has suffered damage – perhaps you dropped a heavy weight on it or it was exposed to severe heat – contact the monitor manufacturer for advice on how to proceed.

  On no account attempt to open a monitor case yourself: there is nothing inside that you could possibly 'service' and the residual electrical charge will quite possibly kill you.

Delicate pins can be easily bent by a weighty cable, a loose connection and the passage of time. Always ensure that you screw your monitor cable tightly into the socket.

Vista video issues

One of the more annoying video issues in Windows Vista is when the snazzy, semi-transparent Aero Glass interface won't display. Provided you aren't running the Home Basic Edition, which doesn't include Aero Glass, the problem is usually one of two things: a PC or video card that doesn't have enough power or an incorrect or out-of-date video display driver.

The system requirements for Aero Glass are pretty hefty. You'll need a PC with at least 512MB of RAM and your graphics card needs at least 64MB of memory. It should also be compatible with DirectX 9, Microsoft's graphics system (almost all recent video cards are).

You'll also need a Windows Vista-specific display driver for your graphics card. That's because Vista has a brand new kind of driver technology, known as Windows Display Driver Model (WDDM). If your graphics card was manufactured before Vista was released in 2007, you'll need to pop to the manufacturer's website and download a Vista-specific driver for your hardware. Once that's installed and you've rebooted your system, Aero Glass should appear in all its glory.

That's the idea, anyway, but in reality Aero doesn't always appear even when you've installed the right drivers. To switch it on when it's being reluctant, right-click on the Desktop, choose

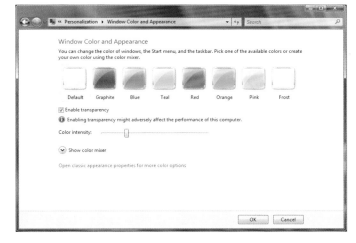

If you've got suitably hefty hardware the Aero Glass interface in Windows Vista is really nice to look at – but if you've got a duff display driver you won't be able to see it.

Personalize and then click on Window Color and Appearance. Checking the Enable Transparency box will turn Aero Glass on.

It's worth mentioning that Aero Glass is quite demanding on your graphics hardware, so if your machine only just meets the minimum system requirements (512MB RAM, 64MB graphics card) you might find that it makes your PC run rather slowly. If that's the case, you can disable Aero Glass by unchecking the transparency box in Window Color and Appearance.

Modem problems

We looked at the ins and outs of a flaky internet connection earlier (p64–68) but here we consider some further possibilities. There are few things more frustrating than failing to get online when you urgently need to check your email or send a message. The best tip of all, of course, is to maintain multiple pay-as-you-go ISP accounts. This way, should one be 'down', you can connect with another and instantly rule out hardware problems. The flipside is that a failure to connect to the internet by any means points either to a hardware fault or to a problem with your telephone line.

Internal modems come as standard equipment on all new computers but external models have some advantages, including portability and helpful status lights.

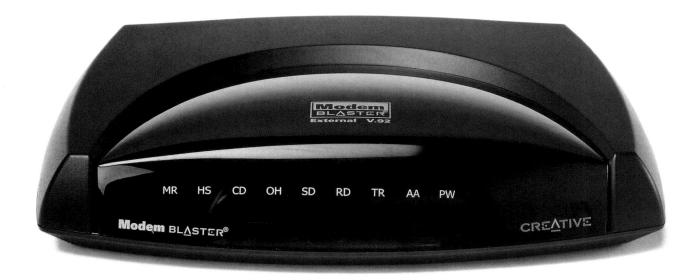

Troubleshooting techniques

● If you recently purchased and installed a fax machine, or even another telephone extension, you may have exceeded the maximum number of devices that can work simultaneously on your telephone circuitry. This is known as the Ringer Equivalence Number, or REN. Unplug the newcomer and try connecting with your modem again.

● When you try to connect to the internet, can you hear your modem going through the motions? This is the easiest way to tell if the number is engaged or if the telephone line is dead.

Turn up the volume control on an external model. If you have an internal expansion card-style modem, the volume is controlled by a software setting. In Windows 9x:

 Start

 Settings

 Control Panel

 Modems

 General tab and drag the slider

In Windows XP:

 Start

 Control Panel

Phone and Modem Options

Modems tab, then highlight your modem

Properties

Modem tab

Now listen for the dial tone followed by the shriek'n'howl response that signals an impending connection. If you get this far, chances are that the ISP is having temporary problems. Keep trying.

If you still can't hear your modem, try ringing your internet access telephone number on a normal telephone. If the number is engaged, keep trying. If you get no response at all, check that you have the right number (see p66–67).

● To check the modem's integrity, try sending a fax with your communications software. If this works, as it should even if you can't connect to the internet, you know that your modem and telephone line are both fine and the problem almost certainly lies with your ISP. To confirm this, try to connect to the internet with an alternative ISP.

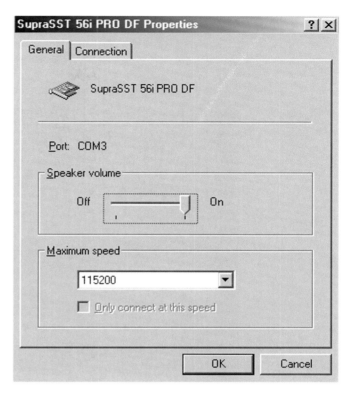

Use this software setting to control the volume on an internal modem.

Fax software can help determine whether your modem and telephone line are both working.

● To investigate your hardware more fully, open Modems from Control Panel as described above. In Windows 9x, your modem should be listed by name in the General tab. Move to the Diagnostic tab to check which COM port it is assigned to (COM 1 and 2 are the computer's external serial sockets; COM 3 and 4, if present, are connections typically used by internal modems). Highlight the appropriate port and click More Info. Windows will now attempt to make contact with the modem.

If you see a *Port already open* warning, this would indicate that a software program has grabbed and refused to release the modem. A reboot will likely solve the problem. A complete failure to communicate means that the modem is, from Windows' perspective at least, effectively non-existent. Reinstalling the drivers may help.

Windows XP has a slightly different route to a similar end. Browse to Phone and Modems Options as described above, open the Modems tab, click Properties and then open the Diagnostics tab. Click the Query Modem button and Windows will check that the modem is present and, in principle at least, functioning.

Some internal modems are set up to use COM 2 by default, which effectively duplicates the second physical serial port. Not surprisingly, this can throw Windows into confusion. The easiest way out of this pickle is to disable the serial port. Not, we hasten to add, with pliers, but with BIOS (see Appendix 1).

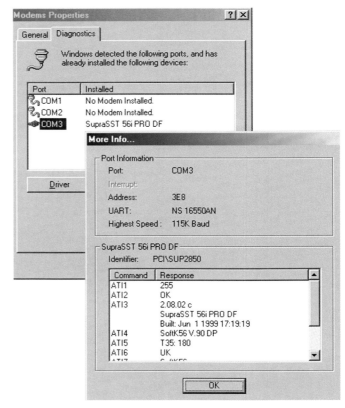

If Windows fails to communicate with the modem, this indicates a hardware or driver error.

● If these tests fail and the modem can't be contacted by Windows, try updating or reinstalling the drivers with Device Manager. Alternatively, uninstall it as described in the sound card section earlier (see p100).

Windows should automatically detect a PCI-based internal modem or a USB-connected external model when you restart the computer; if not, double-check your connections. With an internal modem, this will mean looking under the covers. Moving it from one slot to another may help. However, Windows won't automatically detect an ISA-based modem or one connected to an external serial port, in which case you should uninstall the modem in Device Manager and then manually install the drivers. (We would usually recommend that you check the manufacturer's website for updated drivers at this point but, with your modem out of action and the internet out of reach, this might prove rather tricky.)

Use Device Manager to update drivers or uninstall a malfunctioning modem.

Optical drives

In our experience, CD-ROM drives tend to work pretty much faultlessly pretty much forever – or not work at all right from the off. DVD drives can be a little more temperamental and recordable CD and DVD drives more so still.

Recordable CD and DVD drives tend to be more problematic than their read-only brethren.

Troubleshooting techniques

- Should you get a disk stuck in the drive and the tray eject button fails to work, try opening the tray from within Windows. Double-click My Computer, right-click the drive icon and select Eject from the menu.

  No luck? Reboot and try again. If that still doesn't work, straighten a paperclip and poke it into the tray release hole on the drive fascia. That should do the trick for sure.

Use Windows Explorer to open a drive and eject a disc.

A humble paper clip comes to the rescue when technology lets you down.

- If you find that you can't read a data CD burned on your computer on a different system, chances are you created a multisession disc and left it 'open'. Be sure to 'close' the disc for maximum compatibility. Your CD burning software will have this option.

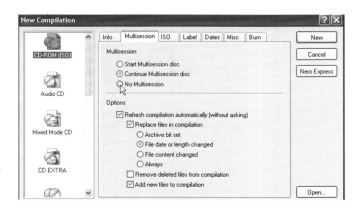

You fill a CD in several stages in multisession mode but it will only be usable when you finish, or 'close', the project.

- Similarly, when you make a music CD, your software may offer a choice between audio or MP3 (or WMA) discs. Bear in mind that only audio discs will play in standard CD players and computers alike, whereas MP3 discs will only play in computers (and some DVD players). Also avoid using CD-RW media for audio discs, as many older CD players, particularly in-car models, can't read them.

You can squeeze hours of music on to an MP3 CD but you won't be able to play it in a standard CD player.

- If your recordable drive keeps spitting out incomplete, and thus ruined, CD-R discs, 'buffer underrun' may be the problem. Lower the recording speed, close all other computer tasks while recording is in progress, and/or try using a different brand of CD-R. Most new drives now have buffer underrun protection built-in, which will save you a packet in spoiled discs. Also be sure to use discs that are speed-rated for your drive e.g. a CD-R rated at up to 24x speed for recording will fail if you try to burn files at 48x speed.

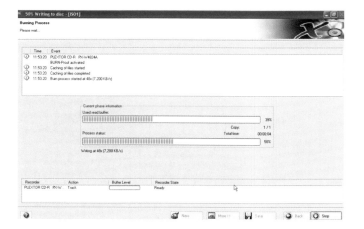

Buffer underrun technology comes in many guises – it is called 'BURN-Proof' here – but all help a recordable CD drive burn successful compilations instead of silver coasters.

- Do you find that you can't start your computer from a bootable CD? Ensure that the BIOS program is configured to boot from the CD drive before the hard drive (see Appendix 1).

- If a CD jumps or skips, try cleaning it with a soft cloth. For a more aggressive approach that can replenish badly damaged discs, use a product like SkipDoctor. This skims off a surface layer to remove scratches and can often resuscitate dead discs.

A scratched CD can (sometimes) be revived with SkipDoctor.

- If your drive stops working but can still be 'seen' by Windows – i.e. it shows up as an icon in My Computer – reboot your computer and try again. Failing this, uninstall the drive in Device Manager (see p100), reboot and allow Windows to detect and install the drive as if it was new hardware. If, however, the drive doesn't appear in My Computer, it is likely that either the internal data or power cable has sprung loose. This will mean opening the covers and experimenting (see p124–138 for details).

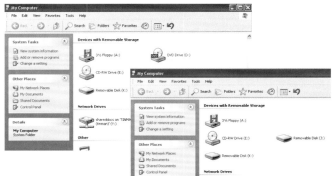

Now you see it ... now you don't. A disappearing drive (D: in this example) means a loose cable.

- Finally, if a recordable drive works just fine in read-only mode – i.e. it can read CDs and/or DVDs – but your recording software refuses to acknowledge or work with it properly, there are two checks to be made.

  First, visit the software developer's website and look for a list of supported drives. You may need to download an update to add support for your particular make and model. Secondly, look for updates on the drive manufacturer's website. Here you may find a firmware download that resolves bugs, improves performance and improves compatibility with recording software.

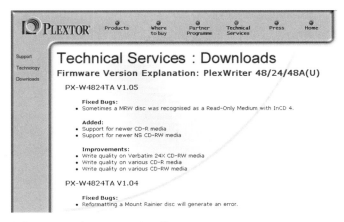

A firmware update can resolve all manner of drive issues. Just be sure to download and install the correct update for your drive.

Hard drive hassles

In 97.3%[1] of cases where a computer persistently fails to start normally, or at all, the cause is due to something other than a physical problem with the hard drive. This means that it makes more sense to run through the full gamut of options first before assuming the worst. However, should you have good reason to suspect an ailing drive, here is what to do.

Under the covers, a hard disk drive is a complex and quite remarkable device. More remarkable still is that they tend to work faultlessly year after year.

[1] A figure we just made up.

Troubleshooting techniques

- If the computer refuses to recognise or detect the hard drive – that is, if you get a complete boot failure – restart the computer with a Windows start-up floppy disk (see p21). Change the drive boot priority in BIOS first if necessary. Now see whether it is possible to access the hard drive directly without going through Windows. At the command prompt, type *cd c:*. If the prompt changes to *c:*, type *dir*. You should see a list of top-level files on your hard drive, including the Windows folder. This tells you that the drive itself is mechanically sound. Work through Part One for options, as the problem is almost certainly a Windows woe.

```
    Award Modular BIOS v4.51PG, An Energy Star Ally
    Copyright (C) 1984-2002, Award Software, Inc.

    Award Plug and Play BIOS Extension v1.0A
    Copyright (C) 2002, Award Software, Inc.
      Detecting IDE Primary Master ... [FAILED]
```

Hard drive failures are blessedly rare and more likely to be caused by a loose connection than an electronic fault.

- Rather more drastically, install the hard drive as a slave device in a different computer. This generally involves changing the jumpers to the 'slave' position (see p148) and attaching it to the second plug on the master drive's data cable. There is no need to physically install the drive in a drive bay, incidentally; the point is just to see whether a different, working computer can read from the drive. If so, take this opportunity to make a backup copy of your important folders, files, emails, contacts and so forth now – just in case it fails next time around. You might also make a disk image which could be used to restore your computer later if you need to install a new, clean drive.

Here, a suspect hard drive has been temporarily installed as the slave device on a second computer. So long as it is visible in My Computer, it should be possible to retrieve and back up files.

● A good option for eliminating faults is installing the hard drive as the master device on the primary IDE/ATA channel (IDE1) in a second computer. If it boots in this environment, this tells you that the drive is sound and the fault must lie with some other component in your system, probably the data cable or PSU power supply cable or, just possibly, the interface on the motherboard.

To eliminate this last possibility, try installing the drive as the master, and sole, device on the secondary channel (IDE2) in your computer, leaving the primary channel free. If it now boots, you have successfully pinpointed a motherboard IDE/ATA socket fault.

This isn't necessarily terminal, as you could install a CD drive as the slave device on the same channel and carry on working.

In extremis, disconnect the hard drive from the primary motherboard channel (IDE 1) and install it as the master device on the secondary channel (IDE 2). This helps you establish or eliminate an interface failure.

● A further option is borrowing a working hard drive from another computer and temporarily installing it as the master device on IDE 1 in your troublesome system. If the computer now boots from this drive, you know that your motherboard, PSU and data cables are all functioning fine and the fault must lie with the original hard drive.

One important note: if the borrowed drive has Windows XP installed, it will need to be 'reactivated' with Microsoft as soon as it is reinstalled in its original home. Booting it even once in a different hardware environment is sufficient to trigger Windows XP's built-in anti-piracy system.

If the worst comes to the worst and your hard drive won't boot and can't be accessed in either your main computer or a second system, there is nothing for it but to buy a new drive and start afresh. However, a recent disk image (p117) will let you recover most of your files and settings. It may also be possible to retrieve some or all files from a thoroughly defunct disk, but you will need the services of a data recovery specialist (see Appendix 2).

Danger signs

There are only three rules when it comes to impending hard drive failure: back up everything now; don't turn off your computer until you have done so (lest it never starts again); and be prepared to replace your hard drive with a new one.

The problem, of course, is knowing when your hard drive is about to fail – and the answer, disappointingly, is that in all likelihood you won't. However, if your drive starts squeaking, clunking or emitting other odd noises, work on the assumption that it may be about to die.

If both your drive and motherboard support Self-Monitoring Analysis and Reporting Technology (SMART), you may get an early warning in the event of mechanical failure and so be able to act quickly. Check your hardware manuals for details. Alternatively, a SMART-capable drive will usually work with drive-monitoring software even if the motherboard has no native support for the technology. Such software is typically incorporated within utility suites, but you can also download a free evaluation version of Ontrack's Data Advisor from **www.ontrack.co.uk/freesoftware/freesoftware.asp.**

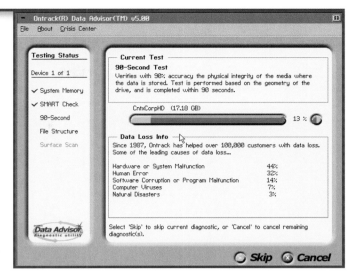

A diagnostic program like Data Advisor can analyse an ailing drive.

Hard disk imaging

A hard disk image file is an exact copy of an entire hard disk or hard disk partition (i.e. a self-contained sub-division of a disk). Should your hard drive fail and you have to install a new one, you can restore every last bit and byte of data from an image file, including Windows, installed programs, personal settings and files. Making regular images is thus the ultimate backup regime and an approach that we thoroughly recommend.

However, a disk image will also contain any errors on the original and is, therefore, of limited use if files have been corrupted, a virus is present or Windows is not working well for other reasons. However, even a wobbly recovery is better than no recovery at all.

Keep image files somewhere safe and remote from your computer (e.g. on removable media like CD-R discs); and use the right tool for the job. On this last point, you really do need third-party software. The market leaders are DriveImage and Norton Ghost, both available from **www.symantec.com.**

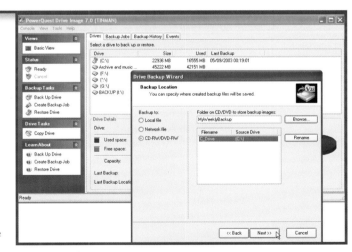

A recent disk image lets you recover from a hard drive disaster.

4

How to handle a dead computer

One of the most disconcerting, even alarming occurrences in everyday computer use is when the infernal machine decides not to start at all. At such moments, one's thoughts turn inexorably to backup regimes (or lack thereof), our reliance upon email, and the prospect of life, if only for a few hours, without access to files and the internet. Like television, the morning newspaper and a hundred other conveniences, a personal computer is often taken for granted – and how our hearts stutter when it fails to function.

PART 4 A quick once-over

When your computer breaks down, your very first
question should be: why has this just happened? Of
course, this may well not be your first reaction in the real
world when you push the big button and nothing
happens – blind panic and bad language are liable to
spring to your mind and lips respectively – but take a
step back, sit down quietly and reflect upon the situation
logically. Computers don't stop working on a whim, so
what could be the cause?

We begin here with a short but essential checklist and then
describe how to strip down a system to its core. Sometimes this
is the only way to uncover a deep-rooted fault.

- A computer checks for the presence of a working keyboard
  during the boot procedure and will sometimes not proceed if it
  detects a problem. Alternatively, you may see a *Keyboard not
  present* or similar error message on screen. This would be a
  sure sign of trouble with either the keyboard itself or, less
  likely, the PS/2 port to which it is connected. Disconnect the
  keyboard, check the plug and socket for damage, reconnect it
  carefully and restart the computer.

  Also look for obvious physical symptoms. Is there anything
  resting on or disturbing the keyboard? Is a key stuck in the
  depressed position? Could the keyboard have been subject to
  a recent spillage?

*Something as innocuous as a mug
handle depressing a key can stop a
booting computer in its tracks.*

● If the power supply unit (PSU) has an on/off switch, check whether it has inadvertently been flicked to the off position. It may also have a voltage control, in which case it should be set to the correct voltage for your region (220/240V in the UK).

Power supplies are generally best left alone but do check the on/off and voltage switches, just in case.

● If you use a gangplank, a UPS (Uninterruptible Power Supply) unit, an adapter plug or anything else between the computer and the mains wall socket, remove this now and plug the computer straight into the socket. If it starts as normal, you know that the fault lies elsewhere.

Alternatively, try using a different power cable. Your monitor is probably powered with an identical three-pin Euro-style cable as the computer so swap them around and see what happens. If the computer's cable works with the monitor, you know it is good; and if it doesn't, it is time for a replacement.

To troubleshoot a power connection, remove all intermediate equipment between the computer and the mains and experiment with a power cable that you know to be good.

● Turn off the computer and give all the connections around the back of the case a gentle jiggle to make sure they are fully home in their respective ports and sockets. Sometimes a bent pin or a temporarily imperfect connection is the extent of a problem.

● Finally, unplug the keyboard, mouse, monitor, speakers, printer and all other devices from the computer. Leave only a power cable that you know to be good connected. Now turn it on again. If there is still no sign of life – and if you are absolutely certain that the mains electricity supply and power cable are both good – then internal exploratory surgery is required. We will undertake this shortly.

First, however, we will assume that the computer does in fact start in this disconnected state.

A bent pin – as shown here on a PS2-style mouse connector – can usually be straightened with fine pliers.

Reconnections

When everything bar the power cable has been removed, you should at the very least hear the whirring of internal fans and a few beeps from the motherboard when you restart your computer. These clues confirm that both the PSU and the motherboard are probably sound.

A little simple trial and error now will help you establish which hardware device is preventing your computer from starting normally. Reconnect one device at a time and restart the computer each time. If and when it stops working, the last device to be reconnected is clearly to blame.

However, you still need to establish whether the fault lies with the device itself or with its connection to the computer e.g. whether you have a duff mouse on your hands or a defective PS/2 port. The key here is substitution testing: connect the suspect device to another computer or connect a device that you know to be working to the troubled computer, or both. If the device is the problem, replace it.

If the port or socket is dodgy – that is, if a known-to-be-good mouse, keyboard, modem or whatever fails to work when connected and/or stops the computer from starting – then you have a trickier dilemma. Short of re-soldering the socket to the motherboard, which we do not recommend, you will have to live without it.

A simple 'hub' can provide additional USB sockets should you need to replace a PS/2, serial or parallel port device.

If this is too great a sacrifice, however, you can easily replace a PS/2-style mouse or keyboard with a USB version, modern printers almost all use the USB interface rather than the parallel port and a serial device like an old modem can be connected to the parallel port with the help of a suitable adapter.

A USB mouse or keyboard can surrogate for a PS/2-style device.

Keyboard diagnostics

Begin by reconnecting the keyboard. As the computer starts, watch it carefully and see whether its three LEDs illuminate temporarily. If so, you know that the motherboard can successfully communicate with the device. If the lights don't come on but you can hear life inside the case, the keyboard itself may need replacing. Now is a good time to conclude that rinsing it under the tap after an earlier coffee spillage has probably done more harm than good.

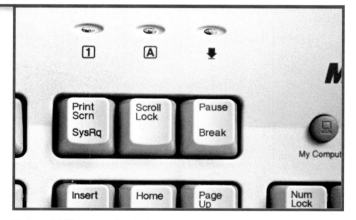

Keyboard LEDs are a simple but effective diagnostic tool. If they flicker on when the computer reboots, you know at the very least that the motherboard is alive.

Monitor diagnostics

Assuming that the keyboard lights do come on, turn off the computer once more, connect the monitor, and reboot. What appears on the monitor screen? If nothing at all, there is a problem with either the monitor or the video card. At this stage, the only way to be sure is by a process of substitution (see p107 and below).

However, let us assume for the moment that the monitor does in fact work and you see POST (Power On Self Test) messages on screen. With the keyboard still connected, restart the computer and press whichever key gets you into the BIOS Setup program: usually F1, F2 or Delete. If you can get this far, you know that the computer is able to boot, which in turn tells you that the motherboard and BIOS are functional and the problem must lie elsewhere: probably with Windows, or possibly with the hard drive. At this point, we refer to you Part One and p114–117.

Off with the hood

If and when all seems truly lifeless – no beeps, no fan noise, no keyboard LED activity, no on-screen images – and you have eliminated faulty power cables, a dodgy keyboard and loose connections, there is nothing for it but to delve a little deeper. But don't be alarmed: even if you have never looked inside a computer before or you are worried about damaging your investment, be reassured that there is nothing much to it. Computers are modular in design and snap together like high-tech Lego. All you need do is establish the cause of the problem and eliminate it, replace it or find a workaround.

Safety precautions

To operate on a computer, you need remarkably few tools. In fact, you can get by with just a cross-head (Phillips) screwdriver and perhaps a pair of pliers. However, we highly recommend a couple of optional extras.

First, an antistatic mat and wrist-strap help ensure that you don't fry components with electrostatic discharge (ESD). This mat is connected to a grounded source like a radiator and you are connected to it in turn with a wrist-strap on a flexible cable (or some such similar arrangement; designs vary). If you don't want to stretch to a mat, at least get a wrist-strap and clip it to an unpainted metal part of the case chassis. And if you really, really don't want to spend a penny on ESD protection, avoid acrylic sweaters and nylon carpets.

A pair of plastic pointy pliers is a must-have accessory for retrieving dropped screws and one of those compressed-air-in-a-can dusters is ideal for blasting away accumulated fluff and debris.

Finally, a small clip-on torch can also be helpful. Big ones are too risky, as you will inevitably prop it precariously on the open chassis while you work and regret this moments later when it falls into the case and cracks the motherboard.

Safety precautions are simple: always unplug the power cable before starting work, give yourself sufficient time, light and space to work comfortably, and keep food, drink, animals and children well away from the action.

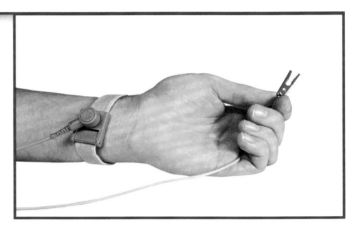

An antistatic wrist-strap is a worthwhile investment that protects your hardware.

Would that all computers yielded their secrets so easily. Be prepared to hunt for a way in.

Covers off

Removing the case cover should be simplicity itself and indeed would be if case designers cared a fig for logic or convenience. You may be lucky and find a couple of big thumbscrews that release the side panels or you may have to prise off the front of the fascia to gain access. Consult your manual, if possible, or root around for clues. Be sure to remove all cables from the case before you begin, including the power cable. There should be no connections between it and anything else aside from antistatic equipment.

A tower case is most accessible when lying on its side with the motherboard flat and to the bottom. A desktop case is fine as is, with the lid removed. Set up your antistatic mat alongside in readiness for liberated components and connect your wrist-strap before reaching inside.

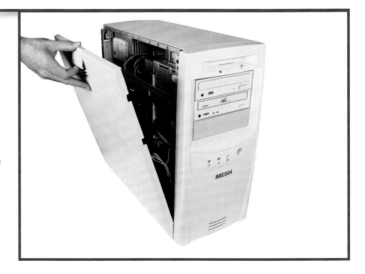

TROUBLESHOOTING

Lay of the land

Before going any further, it is important to familiarise yourself with the internal components and layout of your computer. We look here at a typical tower case design. The thing to remember is that while your computer may at first glance appear to look rather different, it is in fact virtually certain to have the same selection of components. Layouts vary and no two expansion cards are identical in appearance, but you should have no trouble identifying what is what.

3-pin IEC 320 mains power socket

PSU power switch

Integrated motherboard sockets

Expansion cards

Case lock (unusual)

PSU fan

Ventilation grille for internal fan

Cooling unit *A heatsink with an attached fan is designed to keep the processor within acceptable operating temperature limits. The fan is powered by a direct cable connection with the motherboard. The processor itself is attached to a socket on the motherboard, hidden beneath this contraption.*

Drives and drive bays *A computer's drives are usually affixed to an internal shelving arrangement whereby their front panels are accessible through slots in the case's front fascia. Expect to find a floppy drive (on all but the latest computers, at least), a CD drive (probably of the recordable variety) and a DVD drive. The hard drive is the exception because it has no need of outside access.*

Memory *Expect to find between one and four memory modules located in slots on the motherboard.*

Power Supply Unit (PSU) *This unit provides the computer's motherboard, drives and fans with power supplies according to their requirements. The computer's 3-pin power socket with which you connect it to the mains is located on the PSU's sole external-facing panel (to the rear of the case).*

Integrated sockets *All motherboards provide a selection of built-in interfaces, typically including a PS-2, parallel, serial, parallel and USB ports. Optional extras include network and sound ports.*

Case fan *A computer chassis comes with built-in fans to assist the free flow of cool air. Fans are typically powered by a direct cable connection to sockets on the motherboard, although secondary or tertiary fans may use a PSU power cable.*

Expansion cards *An array of plug-in 'cards' or 'boards' provide the computer with additional functionality. A card sits in a slot on the motherboard with its sockets and connections poking out the rear of the case. Typically you might find a video card, a sound card, a modem and perhaps a network card here. The easiest way to identify which card is which is by checking its external connections.*

Front panel connections *A collection of cables that power the case buttons, case lights and case speaker directly from the motherboard.*

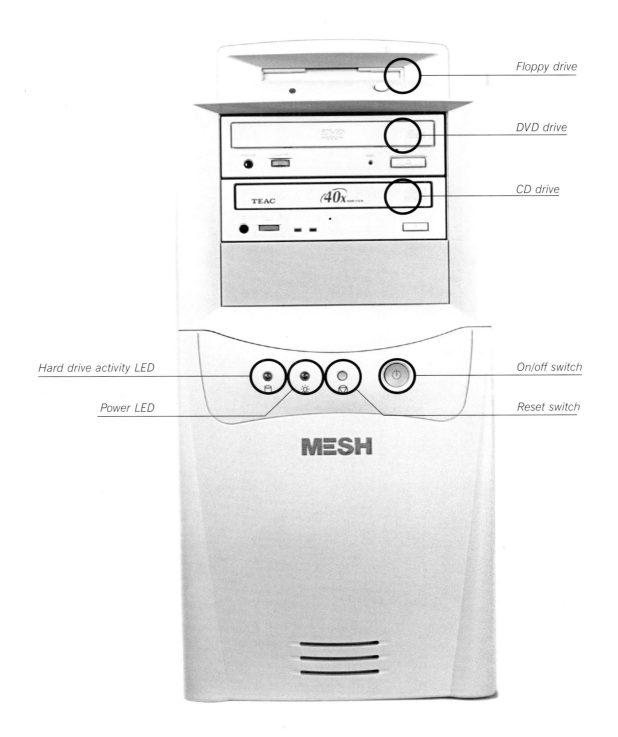

Floppy drive

DVD drive

CD drive

Hard drive activity LED

On/off switch

Power LED

Reset switch

MESH

Motherboard matters

It is far easier to see the layout of a motherboard when stripped of its plug-in components. Here are two to consider.

Front panel
The case buttons, lights and speaker connect here

Floppy interface
The floppy drive connects here

IDE/ATA interface
The hard drive and optical drives connect here

PCI expansion slots
Expansion cards connect here; note that there are no outmoded ISA slots on this motherboard

Power socket *The PSU connects here*

Memory slots
Memory modules connect here

Processor socket
The processor connects here, with a suitable cooling unit secured overhead

AGP slot
The video card connects here

ISA slots *No longer found on modern motherboards, ISA slots were once popular for sound cards and internal modems. The main practical problem with the ISA interface, aside from relatively poor performance, is that it is not plug-and-play i.e. Windows won't automatically detect a new ISA expansion card. ISA cards are also more prone to conflicts with other devices.*

Integrated sockets
A double-height panel of sockets hard-wired to the motherboard
Top row (left to right): **mouse**, **network**, **parallel**, **games/MIDI**
Bottom row (left to right): **keyboard**, **USB** *(x2),* **serial** *(x2),* **audio** *(x3)*

Slotted processor *Note too the ungainly, bulky Pentium II processor installed on this old motherboard. In fact, the processor sits in a slot much like an expansion card, with a heatsink and fan bolted on at the side. All modern processors are flat, square affairs that install in flat, square sockets.*

The inside story

When you are clear about your computer's internal layout, conduct a thorough visual inspection. Work your way around looking for obvious faults. Check that each drive's power cable is securely attached and check that data cables are connected to both the drives and the motherboard. You may have to poke around a bit here and a torch is invaluable.

- All internal case and motherboard fans must be clear of obstacles so watch out for errant cables. Remember that a tower case is normally positioned vertically rather than on its side like this, so look for cables that snag a fan when the computer is righted.

Here, a dangling power cable has made contact with the processor's cooling fan. Should the fan be impeded, the computer would turn itself off automatically – or refuse to start at all – in order to save the processor and motherboard.

- Pay some attention to the front panel array. This is an unbelievably awkward cluster of thin wires and fiddly plugs that together power the case on/off and reset buttons, the status and drive activity lights and the internal speaker. Needless to say, a slipped connection here could render the on/off button inoperable and thus the computer unworkable. You will need your motherboard manual here, or a good deal of trial, error and blind luck, to figure out just where the wires should be connected. Use your plastic pliers with care to test that existing connections are secure and to replace any that have slipped.

The front panel connectors are usually hard to reach and see, but essential nevertheless.

- Examine the memory modules and ensure that retention clips are in place at either end of the slots. Give the processor heatsink a gentle jiggle too, just to establish that it is securely attached, and make sure that the cooling unit's fan cable is plugged into the motherboard.

A loose memory module can wreak havoc with a computer so ensure that they are securely clipped into their slots.

● Many PSUs come with more cables than are actually required. This makes it slightly tricky to establish whether free cables and plugs should in fact be connected to something, somewhere. A motherboard manual is invaluable.

Look for loose connections. Here, the case fan and processor heatsink fan are safely connected to the motherboard side-by-side.

● Press down firmly on each expansion card. If a card drops deeper into the slot, then it was not properly installed and may now start working. Tighten the retention screw that secures the card to the case chassis. If you find that the card springs back up again when you press it home, see p146.

Expansion cards are secured to the case chassis but there may be some room for movement. Ensure that all cards are properly seated in their slots.

● If the PSU fans or fan grilles, internal or external, are thoroughly gunked-up with fluff, clean them carefully. An air duster is ideal for this.

When you are as sure as you can be that everything is in its right place and you have poked and jiggled your way around each component, reconnect the mains power cable to the PSU and turn on the computer once more. If it now whirrs and beeps into life, you should be able to reconnect the keyboard, monitor and mouse and boot successfully. Do not, of course, touch anything inside the case while the power is on.

All being well, power down, reassemble the case, and carry on as if nothing had happened. You would be amazed how often a simple exploratory survey-and-prod procedure like this rectifies a seemingly intractable problem. Indeed, you may never establish the true cause of the problem, but ten-to-one it was a fractionally loose connection.

And if your computer still refuses to start, read on...

It's not pretty and it's not efficient. Clean dusty components with an air duster.

Stripping a system

Here we will proceed on the assumption that a hidden hardware problem is still at play and your computer refuses to start even when shorn of external devices. What we need now is some heavy-duty diagnosis. This essentially means stripping the system to a skeleton and rebuilding it piece-by-piece.

You may find it helps to make notes and sketch a rough schematic diagram, too, or even take digital photographs of the layout.

It is particularly important to note cable configurations. If your computer has two optical drives, for instance, they will likely share the same data cable, and you must ensure that you know which cable connector, or plug, goes to which drive. By all means label cables as you go along, either with a marker pen or with notes attached with tape or paperclips.

If you have a digital camera, take a few close-up snapshots of your computer's innermost parts before you start rooting around. Failing that, make notes and diagrams.

Back to the bones

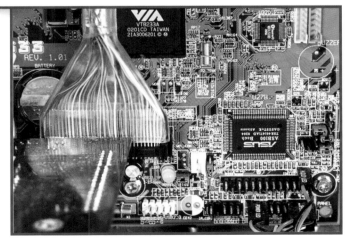

● First, reconnect the mains power cable to the PSU and turn on the computer with the covers off. With any luck, you will see a glowing LED (ATX motherboards only). This tells you that power is getting through, so neither the PSU nor the motherboard itself is lifeless. If there is no LED, you either have an older motherboard or a serious electrical fault. But don't give up quite yet.

ATX motherboards include an LED that confirms whether or not power is getting through from the PSU.

- Turn off the computer and unplug the power cable. Now begin by removing the data cables that connect the hard drive, floppy drive and CD/DVD drives from the motherboard. Look for the red or pink stripe along one edge of each cable and make a written note or diagram of whether this goes to the left or right side of the motherboard socket.

  Leave these cables connected to the drives and allow the loose ends to dangle outside the case, away from fans, vulnerable expansion cards and memory modules.

Label cables as you go along to save confusion later.

- Now disconnect the power cables from the drives. You may have to pull quite firmly to release them, but take particular care with the smaller Berg connector lest you bend the exposed pins on the floppy drive. You don't need to remove any drives from their bays.

  Also unplug any audio cables from the sound card but leave them connected to the CD and/or DVD drives.
  The idea here is to remove each and every connection between a drive and the motherboard, PSU and expansion cards.

Unplug the power cable from each drive to sever the connection with the PSU.

- Now remove the expansion cards (see p144–146 for help with this). Handle each card as little as possible and place it on your antistatic mat immediately. Be particularly careful with the video card as it is likely to have a special retention mechanism that must be released before you can remove the card from the AGP slot.

Protect expansion cards from ESD by resting them on your antistatic mat.

- If your computer has any extension brackets, typically used to provide USB ports on the front of the case or an array of additional audio ports around the rear, unplug these from the motherboard as well. If your motherboard has integrated video – i.e. an onboard chip that processes graphics in place of a separate expansion card – disconnect the port bracket.

Some expansion cards come with separate port brackets, like this sound card. Ensure that all connections with the motherboard, direct or indirect, are severed.

- Finally, if you have more than one memory module installed, remove all but the one located in the first memory slot. This is usually labelled DIMM 1 (but do consult your motherboard manual first).

To minimise the possibility of memory problems, leave only a single module on board. Usually, this must be installed in the DIMM 1 slot.

- When you are through, you will have a motherboard that is completely free of expansion cards and drives. The case fan(s) and front panel cables should remain connected, however, as should the PSU cables that directly power the motherboard. There may be one, two or three of these: see p159 for details.

Be sure to leave the PSU connected to the motherboard.

Three problem possibilities

Let us pause for a moment. What you have here is a computer shorn of accessories. All that remains is a PSU connected to a motherboard and the only active components are a processor and a memory module (or perhaps a pair of modules if your motherboard demands it). But even without drives or expansion cards, it remains a computer, albeit a rather useless one. Fault diagnosis starts here, with three possibilities to eliminate.

● *PSU* Reconnect the mains power cable to the PSU and turn on your computer with the on/off switch. The motherboard LED (if present) should illuminate, as should the power status light on the front of the case. The internal case and processor cooling fans should also whir into life. If not, check the front panel connections for loose cables.

You should also hear a sequence of beeps from the case loudspeaker, probably a single longish beep followed by three shorter beeps. This would indicate a video error i.e. the BIOS recognises that there is no video card or chip connected to the

Check and double-check those front panel connections if the on–off switch fails to function, the power status LED stays dim or the case speaker remains mute.

motherboard, which is just what you would expect. It also rather gratifyingly confirms that the PSU and motherboard are very much alive and that the computer can successfully complete a POST procedure. Again, if there are no beeps, identify and double-check the case speaker cable connection in the front panel array.

If the LEDs stay dark, there are no beeps and the fans don't turn, the PSU is probably faulty and must be replaced.

Unfortunately, a PSU can only operate when it is connected to a load, so there is no easy way to test it outside the case. This also means that a dead motherboard could make a functional PSU appear to be dead simply because no demands are being made of it. A friendly local retailer may be prepared to help with a cast-iron diagnosis.

See p159–160 for help with replacing a PSU.

- *Memory* A faulty memory module can also stop a system at the first hurdle so try swapping the remaining module for one that you removed earlier. If your computer had only a single module to start with, you may have to purchase a spare or two.

The goal is to persuade your computer to complete a successful POST, indicated by a single beep (plus subsequent video error beep codes). If you can achieve this with any particular memory configuration, set the other modules aside for now. You can reinstall them later and establish through trial and error whether one or more causes the system to halt suddenly or behave erratically. See p153–154 for help with replacing memory.

An invisible fault with a single circuit in a single cell on a single memory module can be fatal. Repair is impossible, so be prepared to replace old modules with new.

- *Processor* There are two rather obvious problems if the processor has died: you are most unlikely to have a spare processor lying around with which to exchange the current resident and find out for sure; and the fault may actually lie with the motherboard rather than the processor. In either case, the PSU will probably appear to be lifeless, which is why it is important to rule out PSU problems first.
If the worst comes to the worst and you fear that either the motherboard or processor are indeed defunct – i.e. you can't coax the motherboard into life even with a new PSU connected – once again we would suggest sweet-talking a local computer retailer.

See p161 for help with replacing a processor – or, rather, for advice on why not to bother.

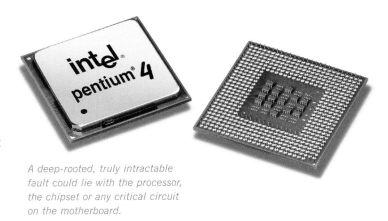

A deep-rooted, truly intractable fault could lie with the processor, the chipset or any critical circuit on the motherboard.

PART 4

TROUBLESHOOTING

Putting it all back together again

Let us assume that the motherboard is alive and the computer beeps at you reassuringly when you turn it on. Leave just a single memory module in place for now, or a pair if your motherboard demands it, and rebuild your computer methodically. If and when the computer stops responding or starts playing up, the cause should be immediately evident. Use the series of guides on p144–160 for help with this as you go along.

When you have reduced your computer to a bare motherboard with nothing but the PSU connected and a lone memory module in place, it's time to rebuild it step-by-step.

It obviously helps to see what is going on so reinstall the video card, or reconnect the video port bracket, and connect a monitor. Reconnect the mains power cable to the PSU and try restarting the computer. Bear in mind that there is no hard drive connected just now so no operating system will load. You should no longer hear the video error beep code that you heard earlier (see p122).

If you do, or if the monitor screen stays blank, it is highly likely that the video card – or, just possibly, the AGP motherboard slot – is at fault. This assumes, of course, that you have already eliminated the possibility of a faulty monitor. One way to find out is to replace the card with another and try again; another is to install the video card in another computer. If you have an old PCI video card to hand, you could try installing that now to eliminate problems with the AGP slot. This is also well worth a try if your motherboard has an integrated video chip and no standalone AGP video card. Remember to tweak the BIOS settings first (see Appendix 1).

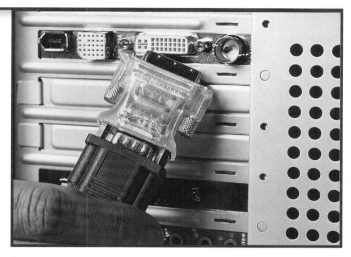

Reconnect the video card or chip at the outset.

All being well, connect the keyboard next and establish that the computer will still start. If so, reboot once more with the reset switch and press the appropriate keyboard key to access the BIOS Setup program (see Appendix 1). Ensure that both the floppy drive and CD drive are listed before the hard drive in the boot priority menu. Save your changes if necessary, turn off the computer and remove the power cable.

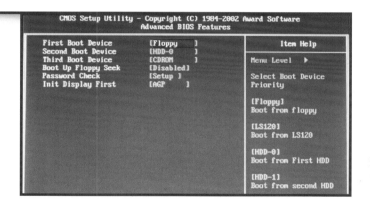

A connected keyboard lets you access your stripped computer's BIOS. Here, the floppy drive is first on the boot list and the CD-ROM drive needs to be shunted up to second place.

Reconnect the floppy drive data cable to the motherboard now, matching the pink or red stripe on the cable with the 'Pin 1' position on the motherboard socket. Pin 1 is simply a reference to the first pin position on a matching cable and interface, the theory being that it ensures the correct orientation of plug to socket (a theory somewhat hampered by hardware manufacturers' inexplicable reluctance to clearly label Pin 1 on their devices). Reconnect the power cable and put a bootable floppy disk in the drive. A Windows start-up disk is ideal – see p21 – but any bootable disk will suffice.

Restart the computer. If the computer can read from the disk, you know that the floppy drive is fine and, more importantly, that the computer is able to boot. Turn it off and remove the floppy disk from the drive.

However, if the computer can't read from the drive, either replace the drive with a new one or test it in a different computer. Or, if you can live without it, remove the floppy drive from the boot list in BIOS and disconnect both the power and data cables.

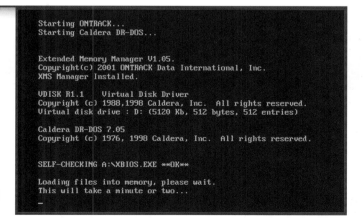

Try booting from the floppy disk. Success here indicates a working device and motherboard interface.

Next, reconnect the CD drive's power cable and reconnect its data cable to the IDE 2 interface on the motherboard. If you have a tower case design, temporarily sit the computer upright on your workspace. If you have two optical drives, leave one disconnected for now.

Restart the computer, place a bootable CD-ROM in the CD drive – a Windows XP installation disk is ideal – and push the reset switch. As soon as you have established that the computer can read from the CD, exit the Setup program and turn off the power. Now reconnect the second optical drive, if present, and repeat the procedure. The computer should be able to boot from either drive. Finally, remove the CD from the second drive and return the case to its prone position for ease of access.

Note that it isn't always possible to boot from older CD drives so don't automatically assume that a boot failure at this stage is terminal.

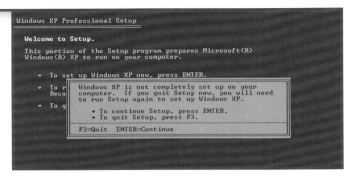

If the computer can boot directly from the CD/DVD drives, this confirms that the drives and the IDE 2 interface on the motherboard are fine. Don't continue with the Windows Setup program at this point!

Having hopefully established that your computer can boot from both the floppy and optical drives, test the hard drive next. Reconnect a Molex-style power cable and reconnect the data cable to the IDE 1 interface on the motherboard.

Restart the computer and look for POST messages on the monitor screen. So long as the hard drive is detected, Windows should load and run. If the hard drive is detected but Windows stalls, consult Part One for options.

If, however, the hard disk is not detected or if the computer fails to start, what to do? For starters, eliminate the possibility of a cable fault. This can be easily achieved by temporarily swapping the hard drive's data cable with the cable for the optical drives. If the drive is now detected, purchase a new 80-wire IDE/ATA data cable and return the borrowed cable to the optical drives. Three other points to check and check again: the stripe on the data cable must match the Pin 1 position on the motherboard socket; the drive should be connected to the IDE 1 socket; and the drive jumpers must be correctly set (see p148

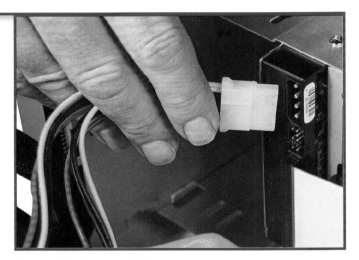

Reconnect the hard drive now and see if the computer starts normally.

). So long as you reconnect the drive in exactly the same way as it was originally connected, these issues shouldn't arise. *For detailed hard drive troubleshooting, see p114–117.*

Assuming that your computer boots and runs Windows from the hard disk, the next stage is to replace all the components that you stripped out earlier. See the guides on p144–160 for help with this and remember to unplug the mains power cable each time.

Reinstall expansion cards in order of importance, replacing them in the motherboard slots from whence they came. As soon as each card is in place, reboot the computer and ensure that it still starts normally. Also visit Device Manager (see p27) and check for newly-flagged conflicts.

If at any point your system halts, you will have identified the problem. Remove the card immediately and check that you can successfully start the computer without it. Note that a short-circuiting device may well blow the fuse in your main power cable, so eliminate this possibility if the computer doesn't restart when the suspect device has been removed (see p121).

Finally, reinstall memory modules one by one. Reboot each time and watch the POST messages carefully to ascertain that the computer correctly identifies its new memory total. That is, the total should rise from, say, 128MB to 256MB when you reintroduce a second 128MB module. If it makes a mistake, or if

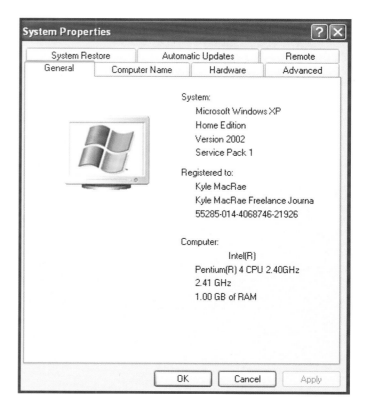

As the computer restarts, the POST procedure tallies installed RAM. Here it is 512288KB (or 512MB i.e. 524288KB divided by 1024).

the computer stops working, starts beeping or otherwise behaves oddly, remove and scrap the faulty module.

As a secondary test, check how Windows interprets the

In this example, Windows correctly identifies 1GB of installed memory.

Common laptop problems

In this section we've concentrated on desktop PCs, but of course laptop computers can encounter hardware problems too. These are some of the most common problems laptop users are likely to experience.

Accidental spills

If you accidentally spill a drink near a desktop computer, the worst you can expect is a broken keyboard. With laptops, though, spills can be fatal – the delicate electronics of your computer are immediately below the keyboard, and if liquid gets in there it can do irreversible and very expensive damage.

Speed is the important thing. Unplug the power cable, shut down the computer, mop up any liquid you can see and then turn the laptop upside down so that the keyboard is facing the ground. Now, leave the laptop in this position in a warm, dry place until all of the liquid has dried. Don't be tempted to turn it on until then.

If you're lucky, quick action will have saved the day – but if your laptop won't boot or does strange things then book it in for repair as soon as possible. Laptop repairers can bring a liquid-soaked laptop back from the dead, but the chance of success decreases dramatically the longer you leave it. Whatever you do, don't wait for weeks – by then, any damage could be irreparable.

Display problems

If the display on your laptop goes dark, it usually means that the backlight of your display – or the circuit that controls it – has failed. However, don't jump to conclusions. Connect the power cable first, because many laptops automatically dim the screen to save energy when running on battery power.

If that doesn't work, the next step is to connect an external monitor. If that works fine, then the problem is almost certainly a little circuit called an inverter, which controls the backlight of your laptop's screen. Replacing this is a job for a specialist, but get a

quote before deciding whether or not to repair it. On older laptops the cost of repairing an inverter might not make economic sense.

Stuck CDs or DVDs

With most PC laptops, you'll usually find that there's a tiny hole in the CD drive just next to the eject button. If you straighten a paperclip and press it into the hole, the CD/DVD drive should pop out and you can retrieve the disc.

Some laptops have slot-loading drives, though, and that's a problem because there's no eject button or paperclip-friendly hole. To remove a stuck disc from a slot-loading system, reboot your machine while pressing the eject key on the keyboard. If that doesn't work, some people recommend using a piece of thin plastic such as a credit card to pop the disc upwards and fish it

out, but doing so runs the risk of ruining the drive altogether.

Unfortunately, in many cases the only way to get a stuck disc out of a slot-loading drive is to take the computer apart, disassemble the optical drive and put it back together again. That's an extremely time-consuming and fiddly job, and once again we'd recommend getting a repairer to do it.

Random shutdowns

Random shutdowns – when your laptop switches itself off without warning – are among the most annoying laptop faults, and they can be caused by all kinds of things including viruses. However, if your anti-virus software says that your system is free from nasties then it's likely to be a hardware problem.

The first thing to check is that the power's connected or your battery's charged, because laptops switch themselves off when the power's running low. If you're sure it's not a power problem, it may be a heat one: most laptops are designed to shut down if they overheat, so if you've been running your machine all day without adequate space around the air vents (or with the laptop lid closed while you use an external monitor) that could be the cause. Ambient temperature makes a difference too: we've noticed our own laptops having the occasional shutdowns on extremely hot days.

If that doesn't work, see if there's a firmware update from the laptop manufacturer's website. Firmware refers to the programs that help your system communicate with its hardware, and it's occasionally updated to fix problems. If a firmware update is available, download and run it (making sure you take a backup first) to see if that fixes the issue.

Once you've exhausted all of these issues you're left with hardware problems: a faulty motherboard, perhaps, or faulty memory. If your computer has two memory modules installed you can test the latter by removing a memory chip and seeing if that solves the problem; if it doesn't, reinstall the other one and remove the second module. If the problem persists, it's time to seek professional help.

Bluetooth buttons that don't do anything

Did it ever do anything? If the answer is no, it's quite possible that you don't have Bluetooth in your system at all. That's because many computer firms use the same model of case for an entire range of laptops, but only some of those laptops actually have Bluetooth circuits installed. Using the same case for machines with and without Bluetooth saves them a few pounds.

If you do have Bluetooth installed and it's stopped working since you upgraded to Windows Vista, device drivers are probably the culprit: head for the manufacturer's website and download the up-to-date drivers, install them and reboot your system.

Disappearing memory

If your laptop is working fine but the amount of installed memory seems to have fallen – so, for example, your system says you have 512MB installed when you know there's a gigabyte in there – then it's possible a memory module has packed up, but it's much more

likely that something's loose. If you tend to take your laptop everywhere, it's possible that the memory modules have worked loose – especially if they haven't been inserted firmly and clipped into place. Turn to Part 5 for a step-by-step guide to opening your laptop, locating the memory slots and making sure they're correctly inserted.

Batteries that won't hold a charge

Older laptops suffer from a problem called battery memory, which is when your battery thinks it's fully charged but it's only partially charged. This is a problem that develops over time, and it's caused by running on battery power but never letting the battery go flat. It doesn't affect modern laptops' lithium-ion batteries, but on older machines with Nickel Cadmium (NiCad) batteries it can dramatically reduce battery life in a very short space of time. You can help prevent this from happening too soon by following a simple routine: every few weeks, disconnect the power cable, use the laptop until it runs completely out of power and then recharge it fully before using it again.

No matter what kind of battery you have, though, its capacity will reduce over time – and in constant use, a battery might need replacing after one or two years. That's because internal chemical changes make the battery less able to hold a charge, and the effects of those changes will be noticeable in about one year.

Power problems

This is usually the fault of a broken or cracked power cable, although occasionally the culprit is the actual power connection on your laptop. If it's the former, a replacement power supply will solve the problem; if it's the latter, your laptop will need its power connector re-soldered or, if you're very, very unlucky, its entire motherboard replaced.

Burning batteries

In 2006 and 2007, major laptop firms recalled their laptop batteries as the internet filled with tales of computers bursting into flames. The fault was traced to a bad batch of Sony batteries, which could, in very rare circumstances, overheat and catch fire. The worldwide recalls happened because the batteries were used by a variety of manufacturers; for example, they were used in Apple laptops as well as Sony ones. It's essential that you keep an eye on your manufacturer's website because battery recalls aren't unusual. If your machine might be affected the manufacturer will provide instructions on how to check whether you have a potentially problematic battery, and if you do they'll replace the battery for free.

If you get your battery replaced under a recall programme, don't assume that there won't be future recalls. In 2006, Toshiba recalled thousands of batteries due to a manufacturing defect and, in July 2007, they announced a second recall – which affected some of the batteries they'd already replaced.

If you discover that your laptop is subject to a battery recall, you should remove the battery immediately and use mains power until your new, safe battery arrives. The risk of something going wrong in the meantime is fairly small but when it comes to the risk of exploding batteries, it's definitely better to be safe than sorry.

Hardware installation guides

Here we show you how to remove and replace key components in your computer. There is really nothing much to it, as long as you take the appropriate safety precautions for both you and your hardware (see p124) and, crucially, remember what goes where when you take things apart.

Expansion cards

As we have seen, expansion cards sit in slots on the motherboard. There are four kinds of slot: ISA, PCI, AGP and PCI Express. The first is now obsolete, the second is used for all manner of cards – modems, wireless adapters, TV tuners and sound cards – and the third and fourth are used exclusively for high-performance video cards.

So long as you replace an expansion card in the same PCI slot, Windows will 'accept' it without question when you reboot. However, if you move it to a different slot, Windows is likely to identify it as 'new' hardware and look for the appropriate drivers. Unless you are trying to eliminate the possibility of a faulty motherboard slot with substitution testing, it is much easier to return a card to its original location.

PCI (left) and AGP (right) expansion cards share the same modular approach to computer construction but use different motherboard interface slots.

To remove an expansion card, first disconnect any internal cables. A sound card may be connected to the CD or DVD drive by means of a thin audio cable, for example. Also note any cables connecting the card to a separate port bracket. The card's faceplate will be attached to the case by means of a screw or retention mechanism. Unscrew or release the mechanism now.

Keep the screw when you free up an expansion card, as you will need it again later.

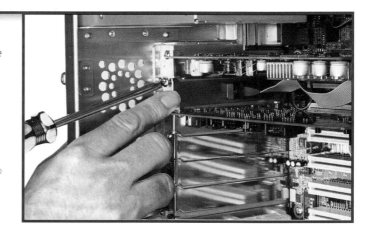

The card can now be lifted vertically from its slot. Be very careful not to interfere with the card's components or circuitry and ideally hold it only by the metal faceplate and the topmost edge. The rear section of an AGP video card is typically secured to the slot with a locking retention mechanism. This must be released as you lift the card from its slot.

Careless fingers can kill capacitors so take it easy here.

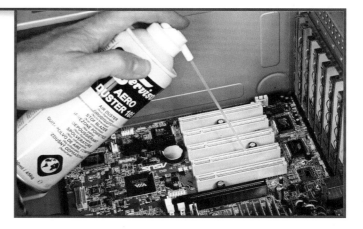

Always lay a card on your antistatic mat immediately, with its components and fan assembly (if present) upwards. Take this opportunity to carefully wipe the card's connecting edge with a lint-free cloth, as dust or grease could cause a short-circuit. Look for any obvious signs of damage. If the card has an onboard fan, make sure that the cable connection is correctly attached.

Handle expansion cards with care – and only while wearing an antistatic wrist-strap.

A squirt of compressed air in the slot is a good idea. This will blast out any resident dust particles. Do not be tempted to blow into a slot, as the moisture in your breath will do more harm than good.

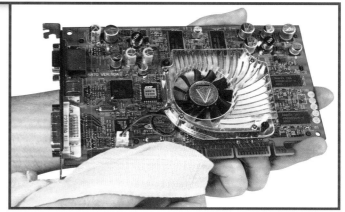

De-fluff expansion slots with an air duster.

To replace an expansion card, simply reverse the procedure. Note that slots are keyed to ensure correct alignment. Align the card with the slot and the opening in the rear of the case and gently push it home vertically into the slot by pressing down on its top edge. Be sure to re-engage the locking mechanism when replacing an AGP video card.

Again, you'll need two hands and a little dexterity to secure an AGP video card in its slot.

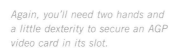

It is tricky to see when working from above but the card must be seated horizontally in the slot, not at an angle. Watch what happens when you screw the card to the case. Does the card remain level? If you find that the innermost end rises up from the slot as you tighten the screw, this would indicate a poor match between the card and your case. This is no minor matter, as a card that isn't fully seated in its slot is unlikely to work properly and may affect the entire system. Stop where you are.

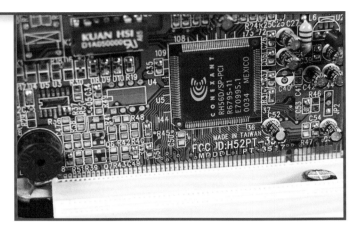

Ensure that cards install horizontally and don't rise from the slot when screwed to the case, as shown here.

The angled L-shaped upper lip of the card's faceplate should – and we stress should – align with the computer case in such a way that a screw (or occasionally a different retention arrangement) holds the card horizontally. Unfortunately, not all expansion cards, motherboards and cases gel together perfectly, and you may have to slightly angle the screw or even squeeze the case slightly to make the connection. It is imperative to keep the card level so, if necessary, keep the screw loose to prevent the card from tilting or find a longer screw.

An infuriating but unfortunately fairly common problem where an expansion card doesn't quite fit the case.

When the card is back in situ, remember to reconnect any internal cables. Also observe the card when you reboot for the first time. If an onboard fan fails to work, switch off the computer at once and re-check the fan's cable connection. Otherwise, so long as Windows doesn't throw up any error messages, you should be safe to continue.

Optical drives commonly connect to the sound card by means of internal audio cables.

If your computer fails to boot or run properly when you reinstall a particular expansion card, try installing that card in a different slot. If necessary, remove another card first to free up a slot. If you do find a dodgy interface on the motherboard – very rare, but not unknown – flag it with some electrical tape to remind you to avoid it in the future. With one slot less to play with, you may find that you can't reinstall your full complement of expansion cards, which makes this a good time to consider USB replacements. Go for the easiest option: an external USB modem, for instance, is a more straightforward substitute than an external sound card.

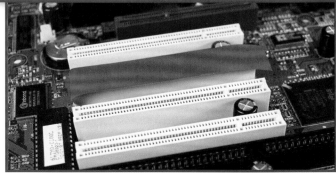

Losing an expansion slot is inconvenient but better that than constant errors or a broken computer.

PART **5** Drives

Floppy disk, hard disk and optical (CD and DVD) drives all slide into bays in the computer case, whereupon they are screwed into place. To free a drive, you unplug the cables and unscrew it from the bay; to reinstall it, you screw it back in again and make the necessary connections. What could be simpler?

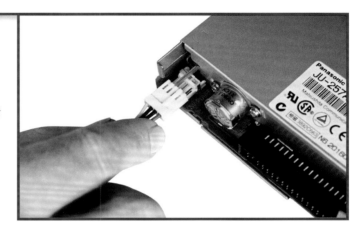

Well, the internal connections could be. A floppy drive uses a 3.5-inch 'Berg' power cable and a special twisted data cable. The power cable must be connected to the drive in the correct orientation, but it is not immediately obvious which way this is. However, remember that the raised lip on the plug goes above rather than under the pins on the drive socket and you shouldn't go wrong. It is possible to connect the cable incorrectly but it requires some force.

Floppy drive pins are easily bent so take care when making the cable connection.

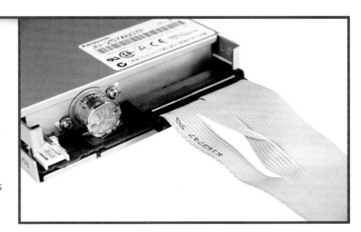

The data cable must be connected with the stripe matching the Pin 1 position on the drive. Check the drive for markings in the first instance – you just might be lucky – or otherwise assume that Pin 1 is the left side of the socket when you look at the drive straight-on from the rear. The motherboard interface may also carry a Pin 1 stamp, but consult the manual to be sure. The floppy drive data cable has a twist in it. The plug nearer the twist goes to the drive and the other end to the floppy controller socket on the motherboard.
In any event, an incorrectly connected data cable won't break the computer but it will stop the drive from working. If the drive's LED stays illuminated continuously, this is a sure-fire clue that you have gone wrong at one end of the cable or the other.

The twist tells you how to connect the cable.

Hard drives and optical drives use a 'Molex' plug and socket. This is shaped to prevent erroneous connections. Data cable plugs and sockets are usually keyed as well – a raised lip on the plug corresponds to an indent on the socket – so it is hard to go wrong.

The typical motherboard has two IDE/ATA 'channels', called primary and secondary and labelled IDE 1 and IDE 2 respectively. The hard drive usually connects to IDE 1 on its own cable whereas two optical drives would typically share a data cable and connect to IDE 2.

Check the motherboard for markings. Here we can see IDE 1 and IDE 2 (poorly) labelled for identification.

The real concern with these hard and optical drives is the fraught and fiddly business of jumper settings. Each motherboard channel can support two drives on a shared cable, but only when one is designated 'master' and the other 'slave'. This designation is controlled by means of tiny plastic 'jumpers' on the drives: little plastic sheaths that slip over metal pins in a variety of patterns to determine the drive's status on the channel.

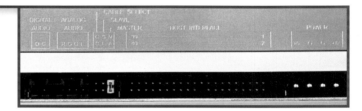

Master and slave settings are controlled here with pins and plastic jumpers.

So long as you reconnect drives to the same IDE socket on the motherboard with the original data cable, you need not worry about jumpers at all. However, if you want to test a drive on a different channel or in a different computer, you may need to change the settings.

The rule is this: if there is only one drive on a channel, it must be configured as the master; if there are two, one must be the master and the other the slave. Unfortunately, there is no single standard governing jumper settings, so check the drive for a guide or consult the manual.

You will also find a handy online database of hard drive settings here: **www.ontrack.com/jumperviewer.**

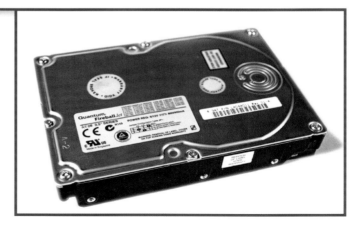

Some, but by no means all, drives carry a handy chart of jumper settings.

Serial ATA (SATA) drives

Many recent PCs use a new kind of technology called Serial ATA, or SATA for short, which makes DVD and hard disk drive connections even easier.

Instead of a wide ribbon cable, SATA cables look more like modem connections. The plug and sockets are shaped so you can't put them in the wrong way. In this photo, we're connecting a SATA DVD drive – we've already connected the power cable as shown on the previous pages.

As you'd expect, the other end of the SATA cable plugs into the motherboard. The connectors are usually easy to spot, as they're colour-coded for easy identification. Once again, the plugs and sockets are shaped so you can't put the cable in the wrong way.

Laptop hard disks

Replacing the hard disk in a laptop isn't particularly difficult, but it's worth considering a few options before reaching for your screwdriver.

Laptop hard disks are smaller (in terms of capacity) and more expensive than desktop ones, and you'll find that it's often cheaper to buy a huge external hard disk and hook it up to a USB port than it is to buy an internal disk that's slightly bigger than the one you've got. For example, at the time of writing, a 100GB drive for our laptop is £150 and gives us 40GB more than we have already, but we can buy a 500GB external hard disk for £88 – and unlike installing a replacement hard disk, there's no danger of damaging the insides of your laptop or invalidating your manufacturer's warranty.

If your laptop has high-speed USB ports, an external hard disk is a better bet, in most cases, than an upgraded internal hard disk. The exceptions are when your hard disk has failed or when you've bought a machine whose hard disk turned out to be far too small.

Know what you need

As you'd expect laptop hard disks are smaller than the equivalent desktop drives, so while a small desktop hard disk is a 3.5" drive, laptop ones are 2.5". However, you can't just buy a 2.5" drive and expect it to work. Older laptops use standard ATA drives, but more recent ones use the newer Serial ATA (SATA) standard. SATA drives won't work with laptops that have ATA interfaces and vice versa. The best way to find out which kind of interface your laptop uses is to check the manufacturer's website, the manual that came with your computer or the BIOS screen when your laptop boots. (For example, we press F2 when the manufacturer's logo appears on our Acer laptop and this takes us in to the system configuration screens that tell us what's installed in our machine.)

Once you know the kind of interface you need, the next thing to look for is capacity and speed. Older drives spin at 4,200 revolutions per minute (rpm) but you can buy drives that spin at 5,400rpm and even 7,200rpm. Generally speaking the higher the rpm, the faster the drive – although you'll often find that there's a trade-off between speed and capacity, so the very biggest drives tend to run at slower speeds unless you're willing to spend several hundred pounds on cutting-edge kit. In most cases, that's a waste of money.

How to do it

Different manufacturers have slightly different approaches – for example, Acer uses a separate plastic cover for the hard disk that makes it easy to locate and upgrade but other firms may require you to remove the entire panel from the base of the laptop – and retaining screws may be in different places, but the actual upgrade process will be identical.

Acer very kindly gives the hard disk its own protective cover and marks it with an icon of a hard disk so you know what it is. You'll find that many recent PC laptops will be similarly upgrade-friendly.

Using a small screwdriver, unscrew the retaining screws holding the plastic cover in place and keep them somewhere safe. Small screws are very hard to find if you drop them on a deep pile carpet.

In addition to the retaining screws, the cover plate is held in place with plastic clips. Lift the cover firmly to disengage the clips and put it to one side.

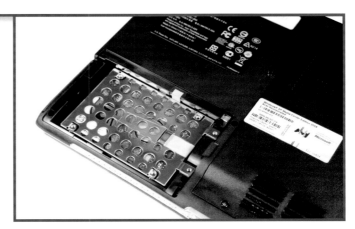

The hard disk is secured with a single screw at the edge furthest away from the centre of the laptop. Remove this screw carefully. Murphy's Law says that once you've unscrewed it, the tiny screw will fall inside the laptop. Simply invert the laptop and give it a very gentle shake to retrieve the screw.

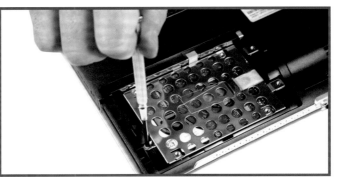

You can now remove the hard disk by carefully sliding it out of its compartment, away from the centre of the laptop.

The hard disk drive is enclosed in a protective metal cage, which is usually secured with two or four little screws. Remove the screws and the cage should simply lift off. Don't lose the screws – you'll need them again in a second.

You now have an empty cage ready for your new hard disk. To fit the replacement, simply follow steps 1 to 6 in reverse: fit the cage, secure it with screws, slide the hard disk into position, secure it and replace the cover.

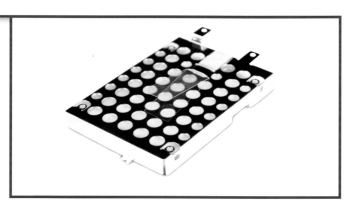

Turn on your PC and put the Windows installation disc (or your boot disc, if you used a program such as Norton Ghost to copy your old drive) into the CD/DVD drive. When the message 'press any key to boot from CD/DVD' appears, press a key and then follow the on-screen instructions to install Windows.

TROUBLESHOOTING

Memory

Memory modules come in all shapes and sizes but plug in to the motherboard in one of three possible slot-style interfaces: SIMM (Single Inline Memory Module), DIMM (Dual Inline Memory Module), and RIMM (Rambus Interface Memory Module). When stripping a system, it helps to reduce the memory to the simplest possible configuration because a lone module is easy to substitute, test and troubleshoot.

A Rambus memory module, which uses the RIMM interface. Most modern computers use DIMM-style modules whereas older computers used the SIMM interface. You can't mix and match, and any given motherboard only supports one type of memory.

In the case of DIMMs, this is no problem: simply leave one module in the slot marked DIMM 1. However, SIMM modules are always (and RIMM modules sometimes) installed in pairs. You also need to install a dummy module, called a Continuity RIMM, in each unused RIMM slot.

In a word, or six, consult the motherboard manual for help. And if you need to buy new memory, use the configuration tools here to ensure that you buy compatible modules:

Crucial Technology   **www.crucial.com/uk**
Kingston Technology   **www.kingston.com/ukroot**

Memory modules can be uninstalled and reinstalled with little effort. The only real problem tends to be geographical i.e. you may find that access to the slots is partially obscured or even blocked by cables and other components. However, retention clips are also rather fiddly, so do take care.

It is possible to be too enthusiastic with retention clips. We, er, snapped this one clean off.

You may find it helps to identify modules with sticky notes (or whatever method you fancy) as you remove them, as they look identical and chances are you'll forget which module was plucked from which slot.

Label your modules as you go along.

Do take it easy here. There is nothing intrinsically difficult about working with memory other than the location of memory slots on the motherboard and the fiddly retention clips.

Note that older SIMM-style memory installs slightly differently to the DIMM procedure described here. SIMM modules are inserted into the slot at a 45-degree angle and then tilted to the vertical. This tilting locks the module into the socket.

As always, ensure that the mains power cable has been removed from the computer and take antistatic precautions (see p124). Release the retention clips holding the module in place and lift it vertically from its slot, taking care not to touch the onboard memory cells. As with expansion cards, clean the connecting edge and give the motherboard slot a squirt of compressed air. Remember to rest modules on your antistatic mat when not in use and handle them as little as possible.

Memory modules are secured in their slots with retention clips at either end.

To replace a module, align its keyed connecting edge with the keyed slot, engage the lower corners with the open retention clips, and press downwards. Again, try not to touch any part of the module apart from the extreme side and top edges. Don't be alarmed to find that you have to press down on the module quite firmly to persuade the clips to lock. Eventually, they should click into place.

It takes a little effort to coax a memory module back into its slot. Ensure that the retention clips are closed before you leave the site.

PART 5 Laptop memory

Replacing or upgrading laptop memory isn't much harder than replacing desktop memory although, inevitably, it's a little more fiddly.

Before you can upgrade your system memory, you need to know two things: what's already in your system, and what you can add to it. Laptops typically only have room for two memory modules, and if both slots are already full you can't simply add memory without having to get rid of one or both of the original modules. Some older laptops won't accept memory unless the chips are identical, which means you can't mix and match different sizes.

In some cases you might find that you can't upgrade your laptop at all. For example, the Dell Inspiron 1000 has a single memory slot with a 256MB chip in it and it doesn't support bigger memory modules – so you're stuck with what's in it. In other cases, you might not be able to upgrade your system by much. Sticking with Dell again, the Inspiron 1100 has two memory slots that support up to 512MB apiece, so you can't install more than 1GB of RAM in total.

The easiest way to find out what's in your system is to use Crucial's memory scanner, which you'll find at **www.crucial.com/uk/systemscanner**. This little program inspects your PC and tells you what memory configuration you have, and it will also tell you what memory you can install.

As with any hardware project the first step is to disconnect the power cable and remove the battery. Our Acer's battery is at the back of the machine. With your fingers, slide the two retaining clips towards the left and right edges of the laptop.

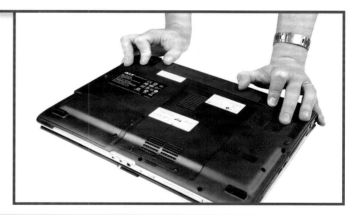

Once you've disengaged the two retaining clips, the battery should slide backwards. If you haven't removed the battery before it might be a little stiff. Remove the battery completely and keep it somewhere handy. Never open up a laptop when the battery is still installed.

The memory slots in the Acer are located near the centre of the machine, protected by a large plastic cover. Unscrew the small retaining screws with a small Phillips screwdriver.

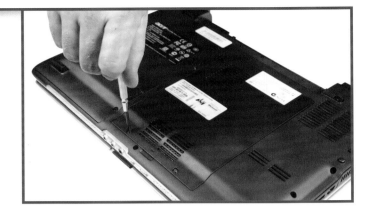

The protective cover is also clipped in place. Using your fingers, lift the edge nearest the centre of the laptop upwards and pull it towards the front edge of the laptop. The cover should now come off. Keep the cover and screws somewhere safe.

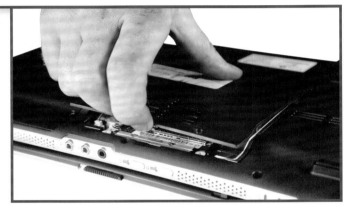

As you can see, removing the cover doesn't just give you access to the memory slots – it also exposes a lot of the computer's innards. You need to be very careful here, because a slip of the fingers could damage something important.

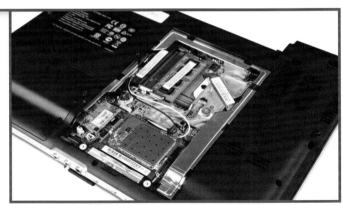

The Acer has two memory slots, one of which is already in use. Line up the new memory module in the empty slot. Once again, both the memory module and the slot are shaped to prevent you from putting the module in back to front.

Push the memory module firmly into its slot. Once it's in place, push down so that the memory module is horizontal. The two retaining clips on either side of the memory slot should lock the memory module firmly in place. If they don't, the module isn't fully inserted.

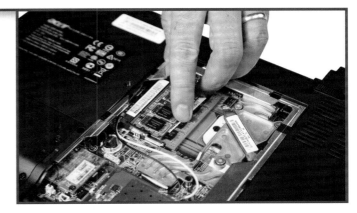

Retrieve the plastic cover and line it up so its tabs fit into the appropriate slots in the laptop case.

Once you've lined up the tabs, gently press down on the cover until it snaps into place. If it doesn't snap easily, check that it's lined up correctly – if it isn't and you push too hard, you could damage the cover, the case or both.

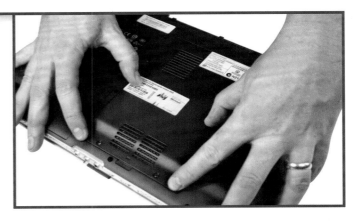

Secure the plastic cover with the retaining screws. Don't overtighten them, though: they're easily damaged.

Now you can put the battery back. Line it up at the back of the laptop and gently slide it into place until the two retaining latches click shut. If the latches don't click shut and the battery is in place, use your fingers to lock the latches. It's very important that these are locked – if they aren't, your battery could fall off again.

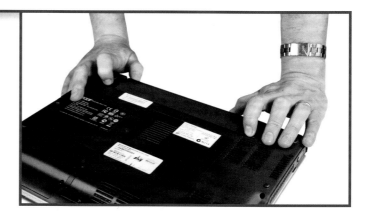

Reconnect the power and switch on your PC. When Windows loads, right-click on My Computer and select Properties. This screen tells you how much memory there is in your system and should reflect the upgraded figure. Remember that if your video card uses system RAM as video memory, you'll see a slightly different figure here; for example, if you have 1GB of installed memory but the video card takes 128MB, Windows will tell you that you have 896MB of installed memory.

In this screenshot, we do indeed have a video card that uses system RAM, so while we've installed extra memory to give us a total of 1GB, Windows says we've only got 766MB. The video card has grabbed the rest of our gigabyte.

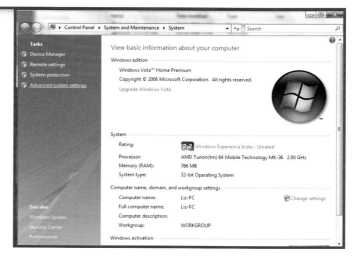

Help! The upgrade hasn't worked!

Once you've installed the new memory and put your laptop back together, you should be able to start your system normally. When Windows loads, right-click on My Computer, choose Properties and the amount of memory listed in the dialog box should reflect the upgrade you've just made.

Nine times out of ten, that's that: your new memory is installed, your computer sees it and everything's groovy. However, sometimes you'll find that your computer doesn't recognise the upgrade, and it's telling you that the amount of installed memory hasn't changed.

Provided of course that you've bought the correct memory and put it in the right place, that means one of two things. Either the new memory is faulty or you haven't fully inserted the memory module(s). The latter is the most likely explanation, so let's fix that.

Shut down the system and disconnect the power cable, remove the battery and re-open the laptop. Remove the memory modules and push them back in firmly until the retaining clips snap into place. If you have to close the clips by hand, you haven't pushed the modules in far enough. Don't feel bad – we've all done it. Once the clips are firmly in place, put everything back together and restart your system. This time, your system should correctly report the amount of installed memory.

If that hasn't fixed the problem, it's possible that the new memory modules are faulty.

PART 5

Power supply unit

If you need to replace your PSU, there are three critical considerations.

● First, ensure that the new model is powerful enough to run your computer. A 300 watt output PSU is the minimum you should consider.

● Secondly, it must be compatible with your motherboard and processor, so be sure to buy a unit explicitly rated for use with an Intel Pentium 4, AMD Athlon XP or whatever processor you happen to have. Ideally, it will have been approved by Intel or AMD.

● Finally, it must have the correct power connections for your motherboard. Assuming you have an ATX system, the PSU should have the following cables and plugs:
  ATX power connector A 20-pin plug that connects to the main power socket on the motherboard.
  ATX Auxiliary An optional 6-pin plug that provides additional power to some but not all motherboards. If the motherboard has no corresponding socket, leave this cable unused.
  ATX 12V A 4-pin plug required by motherboards designed around Intel Pentium 4 processors (but not AMD Athlons). If the motherboard has the socket, you must connect this cable.
  Any computer retailer will be able to advise you correctly.

From left to right, ATX power, ATX Auxiliary and ATX 12V connectors.

Disconnect all cables between the PSU and the motherboard. You may find that one of the case fans is powered directly by the PSU with a pass-through adapter. If so, disconnect this now but make a note to reconnect the fan to the new or repaired PSU later. Also remove any remaining power cables from drives.

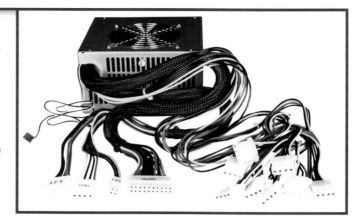

Check that you have disconnected each and every PSU cable from the motherboard and fans before attempting to free the unit from the computer case.

PSUs are usually held in place by four screws. Have a last look for remaining internal connections – the last thing you want to do is wrench an attached PSU from the motherboard or a drive – and carefully unscrew it. Be careful to support the PSU as you unscrew it, as they are heavy and can do substantial damage to a motherboard if dropped. By all means take a non-functioning PSU to a local computer repair shop to see if it can be repaired, but expect to have to buy a new one.

Removing a PSU is a two-handed job if ever there was one.

Replace a PSU in precisely the same way as you removed it, supporting the unit as you screw it into place. Always connect the main power cables to the motherboard first: ATX power and, depending on the motherboard, ATX Auxiliary and ATX 12V. Then reconnect any case fans that use pass-through adapters. Finally, connect 5.25-inch (Molex) and 3.5-inch (Berg) power cables to the computer's drives. Which cable you use doesn't matter at all; just pick an arrangement that minimises clutter as far as possible. For instance, a power cable that splits into two Molex plugs would probably be ideal for neighbouring CD and DVD drives.

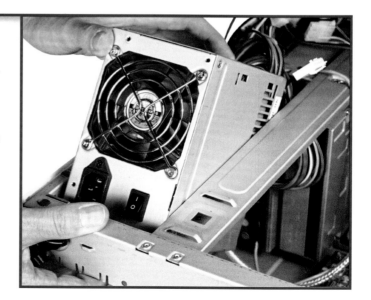

Gently does it. Ease a new PSU into place. The advantage of industry standards is that any ATX-style PSU will fit any ATX-style case.

Processor

Should you need to replace a broken-down or burned-out processor, we offer the following advice.

- Be certain to buy a make and model that is compatible with your motherboard. You need to consider the fitting (the motherboard slot or socket), the manufacturer (Intel or AMD, usually), the model (Pentium 4, Athlon XP, etc.) and the speed rating (don't assume that your motherboard will necessarily accept a faster processor than the old one).

- Only consider 'boxed' or 'retail' processors. These are manufactured for consumers rather than for industry and come with a vitally important heatsink/fan unit in the box.

  If you ignore this advice and intend to reuse the original cooling unit, be sure to replace the thermal material. This is a bond between the base of the heatsink and the processor itself, and without a fresh seal the cooling unit is next to worthless. You can buy thermal grease in a tube or thermal pads that are applied to the heatsink.

A boxed consumer-friendly processor includes a compatible heatsink, fitting instructions and a full guarantee.

- If you have to replace an older model of processor – a Pentium II or III, say – you may be unable to find a boxed product on the shelves. At this point, we would seriously suggest that you consider upgrading to a new motherboard, processor and cooling unit all at the same time. This will almost certainly involve getting new memory, too, as your old modules are unlikely to be compatible with the new motherboard. You should be able to continue to use your current drives and expansion cards, but further research is essential. Some older AGP cards, for example, won't work in new motherboards because the operational voltages are different.

All of which is a long way round to suggesting that a dead processor, particularly one getting on in years, marks a sensible time to think about buying a new computer.

PART **6** **Appendices**

Appendix 1 –
BIOS basics

BIOS – or the Basic Input/Output System – is a motherboard-level set of instructions that kick-starts a computer into life before and quite independently of an operating system like Windows. So long as you can access BIOS, you know that your motherboard is alive.

In general everyday use, the BIOS isn't something that need concern you. However, there are occasions where you may need to change an important setting, usually temporarily.

To enter the BIOS Setup program, you must press a particular key while the computer is booting: usually F1, F2 or Delete. With any luck, the opening screens will prompt you with a helpful *Press DEL to enter Setup* or similarly obvious invitation. Failing that, consult the motherboard manual (or just press F1, F2 and Delete alternately and repeatedly while the computer starts and hope for the best).

This is what we like to see: an obvious invitation into the BIOS.

```
AMIBIOS(C)2001 American Megatrends, Inc.
BIOS Date: 02/19/03 19:39:18  Ver: 08.00.02

Press DEL to run Setup
Checking NVRAM..

255MB OK
```

Once in the BIOS Setup program, explore each section until you find the appropriate settings, and make and save the relevant change(s). Saving changes is paramount here: if you merely exit BIOS Setup without explicitly saving a change, it will have no effect.

Remember to save your changes when you exit the BIOS Setup program.

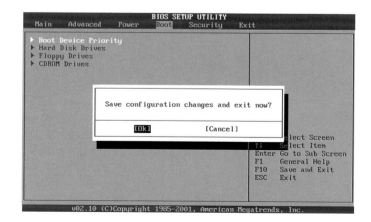

When the computer reboots, the newly-customised BIOS settings take over. You can re-enter BIOS Setup at any time to reverse changes or make further adjustments.

In the course of this manual, there are four occasions when a BIOS tweak may be called for:

● To change the drive boot priority order. This tells the computer to look for a bootable program in any or all of the floppy, CD or hard drives, in the order that you specify. If you want to boot from a floppy disk, you would designate the floppy drive as the first in the queue; to boot from a CD, promote the CD drive to pole position.

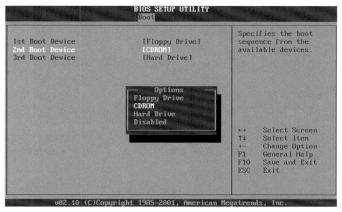

Reorder drives to determine which the computer will attempt to boot from first.

● To disable an integrated audio chip in favour of a sound card (or vice versa). This determines whether the computer uses the motherboard's built-in audio chip or a sound card installed in an expansion slot.

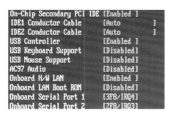

Here an integrated sound chip (AC97) has been disabled in order that a sound card can take over audio responsibilities. Further down the menu is the serial port 2 entry (COM 2), which could be disabled to resolve a conflict with a modem.

● To disable integrated AGP video or the motherboard's integrated AGP slot. This is helpful if you want to connect a monitor to a PCI expansion card rather than an AGP card or integrated chip.

● To disable the serial port COM 2. Only necessary if you run into conflicts with an internal modem.

BIOS may look scary but it is in fact straightforward. Changes are made with the keyboard rather than the mouse so consult the on-screen guide for the required keystrokes. We recommend making and saving only one change at a time, rebooting in between to ensure that the computer still starts and behaves as it should.

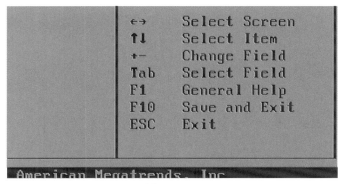

The mouse has no place in BIOS so learn how to use the appropriate keys.

Appendix 2 – Data recovery *in extremis*

Should your hard drive pack in and you don't have a recent image file or backup, all is not quite lost. Specialist data recovery companies can usually save some or even all files even when a device has been subject to electronic, physical or magnetic damage. To put this to the test, we sent a thoroughly defunct drive to Kroll Ontrack data recovery centre. Over a period of several weeks, this drive had grown progressively slower, sometimes taking several minutes to boot into Windows or open a file. One day it refused to boot altogether.

We installed it as the slave device in another computer and tried to access its files. At first, we could see a top-level directory of folders but we couldn't open or copy any files (Windows threw up a frustrating *Drive inaccessible* error message). We then ran Windows XP's error checking diagnostic program and tried again, but still no luck. Nor could we boot the drive when it was installed as the master device in a spare computer. Files were visible but inaccessible.

  Then the drive started clunking, as if it had a screw loose inside.

  And then it died completely.

  We shipped it off to the recovery centre, whereupon Ontrack engineers opened the drive in a controlled environment (essentially a dust-free 'clean room') and established that it had suffered a fatal electronic fault. The drive's internal platters would never spin again.

Ontrack's laboratory for damaged disks.

However, Ontrack managed to extract an image file of the dead disk and ultimately recovered every last file. These were then shipped to us on a series of CD-ROMs and we could restore the entire contents of the dead drive onto its replacement.

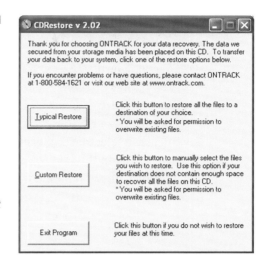

Restoring files assumed to be lost but subsequently recovered is rather satisfying. It is also rather expensive.

So much for the good news. The bad news is that data recovery on this scale is expensive, perhaps prohibitively so. Every job is different and attracts a price that depends on the level of service selected (i.e. how quickly you need your data back), the complexity of the work required and the quality of the recovery, but you would certainly be looking at a high three or even four figure sum.

But what price your data? If you run a small business and your entire customer database goes up in smoke, the prospect of recovery at almost any price will doubtless be attractive.

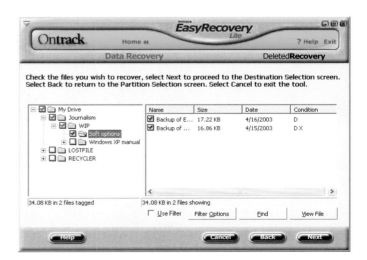

Open-data surgery on a defunct disk.

On a smaller scale, you may be able to recover the odd seemingly lost, corrupted or deleted file yourself so long as the drive is electronically sound. Try the trial version of EasyRecovery from **www.ontrack.co.uk/freesoftware/freesoftware.asp.**

The best thing of all, though, is to make regular backups, preferably with a disk imaging utility.

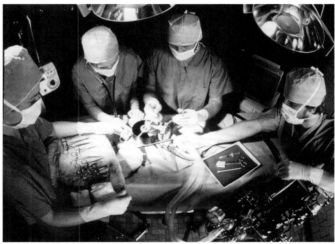

Recover lost files even when you have emptied the Recycle Bin or reformatted the drive (so long as you are quick).

Index

video cards 105–7, 132, 137
video players 70
video problems 49, 70
  see also screen problems
views of a computer 125–7
virtual device drivers 18
virus problems
  anti-virus software 24, 80, 81
  infection 21
  online scanner 86–7
  scanning 84–5
Visual Basic (VB) files 51
volume control, modem 108–9
volume control, system 96, 97–8
VXD files *see* virtual device
  drivers

web page problems 69, 70
web resources 52–6

ZoneAlarm firewall software 81

ACKNOWLEDGEMENTS

Authors	**Kyle MacRae**
	Gary Marshall
Project Manager	**Louise McIntyre**
Design	**Simon Larkin**
Copy editor	**Shena Deuchars**
Page build	**James Robertson**
Photography	**Iain McLean**
Cover photography	**Paul Buckland**
Index	**Shena Deuchars**

The authors would like to extend grateful thanks to
Paul Wardley and Iain McLean for their help with the
preparation of this manual. Thanks are also due to
Sally O'Neill at Lewis PR.